I Chose Me

One Woman's Journey of Healing
After Narcissistic Abuse

Giovanni A. Bass

BK Royston Publishing
Jeffersonville, IN
http://www.bkroystonpublishing.com
bkroystonpublishing@gmail.com

© Copyright – 2025

All Rights Reserved. No part of this book may be reproduced, stored in a retrieval system, or transmitted by any means without the written permission of the author.

Cover Design: BK Royston Publishing

ISBN-13: 978-1-967282-65-4

Printed in the United States of America

Dedication

To my family, who has always supported me in all endeavors, big or small. I truly would not be the man I am today without their love and support. To my clients whom I wrote this book for and who shared their stories with me while we journeyed together to gain strength and get to a better place. And to every person trapped in or recovering from a narcissistic relationship - this book is for you. I see your pain, I understand your confusion, and I know the strength it takes just to make it through the day. My greatest hope is that these pages remind you that healing is possible and that your freedom begins the moment you choose yourself.

Giovanni A. Bass

Acknowledgements

This book is the result of years of counseling and supporting victims of toxic relationships. To every therapist, counselor and coach who dedicate their work to helping survivors of narcissistic abuse - your impact goes far beyond your office walls. Thank you for being safe spaces for people who have to learn how to reclaim themselves and become whole again. To my readers: whether you are just realizing the toxic nature of your relationship or are years into your healing, thank you for trusting me with your time, your attention, your heart, and your hope. I wrote this book for you. May it be an important and crucial tool of empowerment on your journey.

With purpose, gratitude, and hope,
Giovanni A. Bass

Table of Contents

Dedication	iii
Acknowledgements	iv
Introduction	vii

Part One: Understanding the Narcissist

Chapter 1: What Is Narcissism?	1
Chapter 2: The Traits of a Narcissist	19
Chapter 3: The Different Faces of Narcissism	31
Chapter 4: How My Narcissist Affected Me	49

Part Two: Navigating the Relationship

Chapter 5: Recognizing the Red Flags	55
Chapter 6: I Tried to Avoid Setting Boundaries With My Narcissist	65
Chapter 7: How to Communicate with a Narcissist	71

Part Three: Healing and Moving Forward

Chapter 8: It Was Time for Me to Go	77
Chapter 9: It Took Time, but I Recovered from Narcissistic Abuse	81
Chapter 10: No Contact vs. Low Contact	85

Chapter 11: Rebuilding My Life—One Layer at a Time   99

Chapter 12: Now That My Narcissist is Gone, I Am Healing and Thriving   111

Closing Thoughts   117

References   129

About the Author   137

Introduction

How I Discovered What a Narcissist Truly Is

When I first heard the term *narcissist*, I had only a general understanding of what it meant. I assumed it referred to someone self-absorbed, attention-seeking, and overly confident—someone with an inflated sense of self-worth who lacked empathy for others. That definition seemed straightforward enough, then I met one. I fell in love with one. And through that experience, I learned that narcissism goes far beyond arrogance. What I encountered was something much deeper, much more destructive. The relationship affected me so profoundly that I felt compelled to write this book. My intent is not just as a way to process my experience, but as a guide for anyone who finds themselves questioning, second-guessing, or suffering in silence due to someone else's manipulative behavior. My story centers on a romantic partner, but narcissists can take many forms. They may be your partner, parent, sibling, friend, coworker, or even your boss. Regardless of the role they play, the emotional and psychological harm they cause is real. And walking away from them can feel impossible. Truthfully, it's not impossible. Yes, it isn't easy, but it starts with understanding what you're dealing with.

Narcissism, as I came to understand it, is not just a personality trait; it's a damaging psychological pattern that can slowly unravel a person's sense of peace, purpose, and identity. It doesn't just impact romantic relationships. Narcissists show up in families, friendships, workplaces, and communities. Their presence can be charming, even magnetic—at first. But over time, their behavior begins to chip away at your self-esteem, your confidence, and your emotional stability. Narcissists also have very specific emotional needs. They crave admiration, validation, and control. To satisfy these needs, they often engage in behaviors like gaslighting, emotional manipulation, and charm-based deception. Over time, they become experts at presenting themselves as confident, capable, and even generous. Many can fool family members, friends—even therapists. But beneath the surface, their self-worth is fragile. Without a steady supply of praise and attention, their pleasant mask begins to slip. When narcissists don't get what they want, the charming version of them disappears. What remains is someone cold, dismissive, and sometimes cruel. That sharp contrast of shifting from adoration to devaluation is not only confusing but deeply painful. It's part of what psychologists refer to as the **idealization-devaluation-**

discard cycle, which is a typical pattern in narcissistic relationships.

I Chose Me: One Woman's Journey of Healing After Narcissistic Abuse was written to help you understand that cycle. More importantly, it's here to help you break it. Since you're reading this book, there's a good chance you've already been affected by someone who fits the narcissistic description. If so, I want you to know you are not alone, you are not crazy, and most importantly, **you can take your power back**. In this book, you will learn how narcissists think, how they operate, and how to protect yourself from becoming their next emotional casualty. I'll walk you through how to recognize the signs, how to set healthy boundaries, and how to begin the work of healing so you can reclaim your voice and your peace.

You Are Not Alone

One of the most painful aspects of being in a toxic relationship is the isolation. You begin to feel like no one could understand what you're going through. But the truth is—**you are far from alone**. I used to believe I was the only one struggling to make sense of what was happening to me. I thought I was the problem. I felt I needed to try harder, love better, or change something about myself to make things work. But I've come to realize that many people—far more than we tend to talk about—have been affected by narcissists. These are individuals who drain your energy, destabilize your emotions, and slowly dismantle your confidence.

My experience with a narcissist reintroduced me to something I hadn't felt in a long time: **self-doubt**. He had a way of making me feel like I was never quite enough—never doing or being the right thing to make him happy. The confusion, the second-guessing, the emotional dependency didn't happen all at once. It built up over time, through subtle manipulations and constant shifts in how he treated me. If any of this sounds familiar, I want you to know: **this book is for you**. It will help you identify the signs of narcissistic behavior. It will show you the mental and emotional games narcissists often play. And most importantly, it will help you **reclaim your sense of self**, which is usually the first thing lost in a narcissistic relationship.

What You'll Find in This Book
We're going to explore the different types of narcissists because not all of them look or act the same. Some are loud

and overt, others are quiet but just as destructive. You'll learn about the emotional damage narcissists inflict, how to manage your interactions with them, and how to rebuild your boundaries. I'll also share how I personally worked through the aftermath and how I began to **reclaim my power,** enabling me to move forward with clarity, strength, and self-respect.

This book is for you if:
- You've been gaslighted, manipulated, or emotionally exhausted by someone in your life
- You've experienced extreme highs and lows in a relationship and couldn't understand why
- You struggle to assert yourself around a controlling or emotionally dominant person
- You've received constant criticism from someone close to you, and it's worn away your confidence
- You've asked yourself, *"Am I the crazy one?"* because their version of reality constantly overrides yours
- You feel stuck in a toxic dynamic and don't know how to leave—or even if you can

Why This Matters Now

It may feel like narcissists are everywhere these days—and in some ways, they are. You'll find them in romantic relationships, families, friendships, workplaces, and even leadership positions. The emotional toll they take can be long-lasting. Their influence can lead to chronic stress, anxiety, depression, and a fractured sense of identity. However, here's the good news: Once you recognize the patterns, you can break free from them. The more you learn about how narcissists operate, the less power they have over you. This book is your guide—not just to understanding the narcissist in your life, but to rediscovering the parts of yourself you may have lost along the way.

Chapter 1
What Is Narcissism?

An Overview of Narcissistic Personality Disorder (NPD)
Narcissism is often misunderstood. It's more than just arrogance or vanity; it's a deeply rooted personality pattern driven by an intense need for admiration, an exaggerated sense of self-importance, and a lack of empathy for others. This behavior can be especially damaging when it comes from someone close who you love, trust, or depend on.

In my case, the narcissist I was involved with had an overwhelming belief that he was superior to me and everyone around him. He expected special treatment in every situation. I remember countless times we'd go out to eat, and if the staff didn't cater to him in the way he felt he deserved, we'd leave the restaurant with him criticizing the service, the food, and the atmosphere. And if I didn't agree with his harsh assessment, that disagreement would escalate into an argument that could last hours. It was exhausting.

Over time, I began to see how fragile his confidence was. Despite the surface-level arrogance, his self-esteem was dependent on constant external validation. When that validation didn't come, especially from me, his response was often manipulative, angry, or emotionally cruel. I remember the moment I realized how accustomed I had become to the cruelty. That was the moment I knew something was deeply wrong.

Narcissists can be found in every kind of relationship. They aren't limited to romantic partners; they show up in families, friendships, workspaces, and social groups. And they don't fit one mold. Narcissists can be male or female, young or old, loud or quiet. They come from all walks of life and exist in every social class. The one thing they all have in common is this: they know how to pull people in.

In the beginning, narcissists often present themselves as magnetic, confident, and even charming. They make you feel special, seen, and chosen; however, what you're responding to is a performance, not a true connection. Once they feel secure in your trust, they begin to reveal their true nature. Slowly, their focus shifts from bonding with you to **controlling** you. They use confusion, guilt, emotional manipulation, and subtle forms of psychological control to wear down your defenses. Often, by the time you realize what's happening, your sense of self is already compromised.

What many others and I have experienced is not a relationship built on love. It's a relationship built on **emotional dependency**, sustained by cycles of affection and punishment, closeness, and rejection. This is the foundation of Narcissistic Personality Disorder, and the first step in healing is learning how to name what you've been through.

Where Does Narcissism Come From?
At times, it felt like the narcissist in my life had dropped straight out of the sky fully formed and determined to cause emotional chaos. It was as if he had been created solely to challenge my peace. The truth is, narcissists don't just appear out of thin air. Narcissistic behavior develops over time, shaped by a combination of early life experiences, environmental influences, and in some cases, biological or genetic factors. My therapist once explained it this way: "Narcissism is often a defense. It's a psychological shield someone constructs to protect themselves from deep feelings of unworthiness and inadequacy." Hearing that gave me a moment of pause. It made the behavior almost

understandable. For a split second, I wondered if I should feel sorry for him. But here's what I've learned: **you can acknowledge someone's pain without allowing it to destroy you.** You can understand without enabling, and you can empathize without staying.

The Role of Childhood Experiences
Childhood is often where the seeds of narcissism are planted, and there are typically two main developmental paths:

1. Neglect and Emotional Abuse
Some narcissists grow up in emotionally cold or critical environments. They may have had parents who were narcissistic themselves, unavailable, or excessively harsh. As children, they learned to cope with the pain of feeling unseen or unworthy by constructing a false sense of superiority. This *false self* becomes their armor—a grandiose identity designed to mask deep emotional wounds. Over time, that defense becomes their default way of interacting with the world.

2. Over-Praising and Entitlement

Then there's the opposite path marked by excessive praise and indulgence. This was the case with the narcissist I was involved with. He was raised in an environment where he was constantly validated, celebrated, and treated as if he were the center of the universe. He wasn't taught accountability, humility, or how to process emotional discomfort. He was never asked to consider how others felt or to step outside of his own experience. As a result, he carried those expectations into adulthood. He believed others should treat him the same way his parents did by admiring, accommodating, and never challenging him. When I didn't meet those expectations, he couldn't process it. He lacked the emotional tools to engage with empathy or insight. It became painfully clear that he could not genuinely understand or care about how I felt. He just couldn't do it.

The Role of Biology and Genetics

Beyond upbringing, research also suggests that narcissistic traits can be influenced by biology. Some individuals may be born with certain personality traits, such as high extroversion or emotional impulsivity, that increase their likelihood of developing narcissistic behaviors. Genetics can also play a role. According to the field of epigenetics, emotional patterns and personality tendencies can be passed down through generations. Studies have shown that people with Narcissistic Personality Disorder may even have measurable differences in brain structure, particularly in regions associated with empathy, emotional regulation, and self-awareness. Near the end of my relationship, I found myself saying, more out of frustration than anything else, "There has to be something wrong with his brain." And as it turns out, there might have been some neurological inadequacies.

The Influence of Culture and Society
Finally, it's essential to consider the cultural environment we live in today. We're surrounded by messaging that encourages self-promotion, performance, and superficial success. Narcissistic traits are often rewarded—especially in media, celebrity culture, and social media platforms.

A therapist friend of mine once shared an eye-opening insight. He was working with a client who had appeared on reality television, and he explained that many reality shows seek out individuals who test high on traits like narcissism or emotional reactivity. Why? Because it makes for dramatic, attention-grabbing content. Producers understand that people who prioritize image, status, and external validation tend to create tension, and tension keeps viewers hooked.

Young people absorb these messages early. They watch influencers and public figures gain popularity by being provocative, boastful, or self-obsessed. Over time, those behaviors are normalized and even admired. In that kind of environment, it's easy to see how narcissistic tendencies can be reinforced and adopted, especially if someone is already vulnerable to them.

A Dangerous Mix of Factors

Narcissism isn't always the result of one cause. It's usually the product of many causes stemming from emotional wounds, excessive praise, environmental reinforcement, and in some cases, a biological predisposition. No matter how it develops, the outcome is the same: relationships marked by imbalance, manipulation, and emotional harm.

Understanding where narcissism comes from doesn't excuse it, but it does provide clarity, and with clarity comes power. When you know the origin of something, you gain the tools to better protect yourself from it. And that's exactly what the next part of this book is here to help you do.

Which One Did I Have? A Pathological Narcissist or a Healthy Narcissist?

When I first began researching narcissism, I had one overwhelming conclusion: all narcissists are harmful. It was a belief rooted in my own painful experience. As I dug deeper, I came across something that surprised me; **not all narcissism is toxic**. In fact, there's a version of it that can be healthy, even beneficial.

Healthy narcissism is what allows people to carry a sense of self-worth and confidence. It's what pushes someone to pursue goals, believe in their abilities, and stand tall in the face of adversity. Healthy narcissists are not devoid of empathy; they can reflect on their behavior, acknowledge their impact on others, and take accountability. They can be assertive without being aggressive, proud without being condescending, and driven without stepping on others to get ahead. A person with healthy narcissism might be a leader, an entrepreneur, or a creative visionary. These are people who believe in their talents but still value people and tend to contribute to the lives of others. They build rather than destroy.

Pathological narcissism, on the other hand, is an entirely different world. It's rigid, extreme, and deeply damaging. When I first read about it in depth, I had a gut-level reaction: *This is him. This is the man I was entangled with.* At the beginning, I couldn't see it. I was swept up in the charm and intensity of his love bombing. He made me feel seen, cherished, and chosen. However, over time, I realized it was always going to be his way or no way at all. By the time I truly saw the signs for what they were, I was already emotionally invested. I told myself he was complicated, misunderstood, even brilliant. What I had to accept slowly and painfully was that he only engaged in relationships where he had something to gain. Everything was transactional. That included me. I wasn't an exception. I was just part of the pattern. Coming to terms with that was gut-wrenching.

One of the defining traits of a pathological narcissist is that they cannot tolerate criticism. None. Zero. Even when they pretend to take it in stride, they are filing it away and waiting for the right moment to retaliate, and my guy did, repeatedly. If I said something he didn't like, he would punish me emotionally for weeks. I wasn't prepared for how persistent the backlash would be. It wasn't just a disagreement; it became a drawn-out campaign to make me regret ever opening my mouth. He'd say things like, *"You don't respect me"* or *"You don't see me as a man."* The truth is, I had respected him. I had never questioned his manhood. I had only tried to express my needs. That, to him, was a threat.

He, on the other hand, could criticize me without limits. He found fault with everything from how I talked to how I dressed to the way I lived. And no matter how painful his words were, I found myself trying to explain, trying to reason, trying to keep the peace. The imbalance was exhausting.

Eventually, I came to recognize the pattern—**the cycle of idealization, devaluation, and discard**. It's a familiar dynamic in narcissistic relationships. In hindsight, I can see each stage clearly. At the time, though, I was too deep inside the emotional fog to make sense of what was happening. Understanding that pattern gave me language for what I'd experienced. It gave me clarity, and with that clarity came the power to begin separating from him—not just physically, but mentally and emotionally as well. That's where healing truly begins.

The Idealization Phase
I met him at a local runner's club. From the beginning, there was a mutual awareness between us—one of those quiet recognitions that doesn't need to be spoken aloud. Still, we kept it professional at first. We were there to run, and that's exactly what we did. I remember the early days so clearly. I would glance at him during our runs, and he would glance back. Just simple exchanges at first—fleeting smiles, shared breath, silence. At the time, I had just come out of a serious relationship that had ended because of betrayal. Infidelity has a way of wounding you deeply, and I told myself I wasn't ready to meet anyone new. I needed time—for reflection, for healing, for solitude. What I didn't fully realize then was just how vulnerable I was. I thought I was strong. I thought my decision to leave that previous relationship meant I was grounded and self-aware. What I've come to understand is that **no matter how courageous your exit may be, heartbreak leaves invisible fractures.** And unless you give yourself the time and space to mend,

those fractures can pull you back into something equally damaging, if not worse.

Narcissists have an uncanny ability to read people. They can scan your emotional state like a radar. And when they sense vulnerability, they adjust themselves accordingly. They mirror your needs, your pace, your energy. It's not connection they're after—it's control, and they disguise it well. They don't come at you with demands or declarations. Instead, they observe, they study, and then they present exactly what you think you need.

Looking back, it's clear he recognized two things about me right away: that I was kind, and that I was emotionally open. Narcissists are often drawn to people with empathy—people who listen, give, trust, and forgive. It creates the perfect dynamic for imbalance. You usually see this in mismatched couples: one partner warm and emotionally generous, the other detached, cold, and self-focused. That was us; however, I didn't know it yet.

In the beginning, he was attentive in ways I hadn't experienced before. He poured out affection, compliments, and acts of service. He seemed invested. Present.

Thoughtful. He made me feel like I mattered. It was not just in a romantic way, but in a profound, life-altering way. It felt like I had finally met someone who truly saw me. What I didn't understand then was that this intense outpouring of attention wasn't authentic—it was a calculated strategy. **It was love bombing,** a hallmark of the idealization phase. Narcissists do this to create emotional dependency. They build you up rapidly, making you feel like you're the center of their universe. And once you're emotionally anchored, the dynamic shifts. By the time I saw it for what it really was, I was already in love.

The Devaluation Phase

Looking back, it's almost eerie how swiftly things shifted. It felt like the very week I admitted to myself that I was in love with him, he began the process of unraveling me. It started with a seemingly harmless comment—about my hair. He said, almost casually, *"I don't know why you always wear your hair that way. It's the same thing every day."* The words landed sharply, piercing through a deep personal insecurity. Hair, for me, wasn't just about appearance—it was tied to legacy and loss. Women in my family experience hair thinning and balding as they age. I had developed my style out of both comfort and quiet resilience. So his criticism felt unusually cruel. I brushed it off. At the time, I told myself it was a one-time slip, a careless remark. I had no idea it was the beginning of a pattern. Soon after, I began noticing other minor changes. He started keeping his phone facedown around me—a stark contrast to the openness he displayed at the beginning. When we first met, his cellphone was face-up, unlocked, unguarded. Now, it was hidden, guarded, and out of reach. I told myself not to overthink it. I didn't want to seem paranoid or controlling. Deep down, I was starting to feel something wasn't right.

There were clear red flags, and I ignored them. I didn't want to believe they meant anything; I learned the hard way. **Red flags are never meaningless. They're warnings, and they always deserve your respect.** Eventually, the weight of those flags became too heavy to carry silently. I began speaking up, asking questions, and expressing concern. That's when the gaslighting started. I remember one moment in particular: I saw a message flash across his screen. It was flirtatious, filled with heart emojis—clear and unmistakable. When I asked him about it, he denied everything. Not only did he say he never received a message, he insisted that I must have imagined the entire thing. We argued for hours, and by the end, I found myself questioning my memory and perception. That's how gaslighting works. It isn't always dramatic or loud—it's quiet, methodical, and deeply destabilizing. Over time, it strips you of your ability to trust your instincts. And once that's gone, you become easier to control.

Once he gained that psychological advantage, his true nature emerged more boldly. The criticisms came more frequently. So did the passive-aggressive behaviors—the subtle jabs, the silent treatments, the withdrawal of affection. Even things as petty as leaving the toilet seat up became symbols of disregard. These weren't random slips; they were intentional. They didn't start until he was sure of one thing: that I was emotionally invested. And I was. I stayed longer than I should have, hoping that the man I fell for—the warm, attentive version—would return. But he didn't. He had been replaced by someone cold, calculated, and disturbingly unkind. I remember thinking to myself, *What have I gotten myself into?*

The emotional strain began manifesting in my body. I lost weight rapidly—not because I wanted to, but because my stress levels were unbearable. I couldn't sleep. I avoided mirrors. And yes—my hair began to fall out. The very thing he had mocked became a painful reality. I wanted to reach out to my mother, my aunt, someone who knew me well. By that point, he had already isolated me. He would question me every time I spoke to someone close. He would ask, *"What are you telling them? "Are you lying about me again? No one's going to believe you. Hell, even you don't believe a word you say."*

That line—*"Even you don't believe a word you say"*—landed like a punch to the chest. Because it wasn't just an insult. It was confirmation that he knew exactly what he was doing. He knew I was doubting myself, he knew my confidence had eroded, and he took pride in it. He knew—and he didn't care. By then, my self-worth had almost completely dissolved. I was emotionally worn down, psychologically drained, and physically fragile. The devaluation had worked. He had slowly dismantled me.

The Discard Phase
Eventually, the day came when he decided I was no longer useful to him. And the timing couldn't have been worse. Ironically, I had just begun to find my footing again. I was quietly gathering the strength to walk away, to reclaim my

peace, to rebuild what had been torn down in me. Yet before I could take that step, he decided for both of us.

We argued that day, and in my mind, I had planned to use it as a turning point to finally end the relationship on my terms. But before I could speak, he cut in, his voice sharp and cold. *"Why don't you just get the hell on and go back to wherever you came from?"* The words stunned me. As much as I wanted to leave, I didn't want to be discarded. I didn't want him to have the final word. I didn't want to walk away stripped of my dignity, as if I had been dismissed like I didn't matter. And yet, that's exactly how it felt. I was devastated—not because I loved him, but because I had lost my power in the end. Something strange happened after that. Despite everything I had endured, despite the clear signs that this relationship was toxic and emotionally dangerous, a part of me still wanted to fix it. Still wanted to be chosen. Still wanted to prove I was worthy of the love I once thought we had. And so, I went back.

He let me back in, but not because he cared. It was a cycle; one I would repeat seven, maybe eight times. He would discard me, I would reach out, and he would take me back.

And each time, I returned to a colder version of the man I had once believed in. Each time, it took less and less for him to unravel me all over again. Every return led me back to the same haunting question: *What have I gotten myself into?*

Chapter 2
The Traits of a Narcissist

If we are being realistic, not everyone you meet is a full-blown narcissist. Some people carry strong narcissistic traits that, when unchecked, can still cause serious harm. If you know what to look for early on, it can save you from a world of emotional chaos. I didn't know then what I know now, and honestly, I wish I had. Looking back, the signs were there. Clear as day. I didn't know how to read them. Below are the traits I now understand to be classic red flags—and yes, my ex had all of them.

1. Superiority Complex and Grandiosity
He always had to be the center of attention. This man carried himself like he was the smartest, strongest, fastest person in every room, even when it was painfully obvious he wasn't. He needed people to see him as elite, exceptional, untouchable. At first, I mistook it for confidence. I thought maybe I was dealing with someone who really believed in himself, someone ambitious with a fire under him. But over time, I realized it wasn't confidence—it was delusion. What made it worse was the contrast between who he *thought* he was and who he

actually was. He talked a big game—about his future, his "genius," how he was going to surpass everyone at work and leave all the "idiots" behind. Meanwhile, he wasn't making real moves. He wasn't even financially stable. I had to step in and help him get by, and yet he still acted like the world owed him something.

He couldn't just be proud of himself—he had to tear others down to build himself up. That's how narcissistic grandiosity works. It's not rooted in real achievement; it's rooted in a fragile ego and the constant need to feel superior, even at someone else's expense.

2. Lack of Empathy
He didn't care about how I felt—period. Whether I was tired, anxious, hurting, or heartbroken, it didn't matter. My needs were always too much, and my emotions were an inconvenience. If it didn't concern his emotions or his needs, it didn't count. And what's wild is that I *knew* this kind of energy already. I had grown up around a narcissist, so I recognized that emotional coldness—the inability to see or care about someone else's pain. I just didn't want to believe I had found myself in that same situation again.

3. Constant Need for Validation

He needed praise like he needed air. Every compliment was soaked up, but nothing ever felt like enough. He needed to be reminded daily that he was "the man." The minute he didn't get that attention, his mood would shift. He'd sulk, pout, or lash out in subtle ways. Sadly, I found myself constantly trying to feed his ego to keep the peace. I didn't even realize how much energy I was pouring into keeping him emotionally "okay"—while I was running on empty.

4. Control and Manipulation

He controlled the narrative. If something went wrong, he flipped it on me. If I had a concern, he turned it into a criticism. If I asked a question, he accused me of not trusting him, which was his way of staying in power by constantly shifting blame and planting seeds of self-doubt.

5. Entitlement

He expected things from me as if it were his right; for example, time, money, and emotional labor. I was supposed to show up for him in every way; not once did he ask what I needed. It was a one-way relationship masked as mutual love.

6. Fragile Ego and Sensitivity to Criticism

Ironically, for someone who claimed to be so confident, he couldn't handle even the slightest feedback. I once mentioned something small, something gentle—and he exploded. Not right away, of course. He held it in until he could find the right moment to punish me for it. Meanwhile, he'd criticize me left and right. He would complain about how I dressed, how I spoke, and how I moved. And I let it slide over and over again, thinking maybe if I improved myself, the relationship would get better. It never did.

These were the traits that slowly revealed themselves as our relationship unraveled. And the more I reflect on them now, the more I realize: I saw the red flags. I didn't know how to name them yet. But now I do. And so do you.

He Had No Empathy for Me

I'm the kind of person who feels deeply; when I love someone, I love hard. Because of that, I used to believe that love should be mutual. If I show you care, I expect you to show it back. If I have your back, I expect you to have mine. With a narcissist, that exchange is one-sided. And it hurts deeply.

At first, he *acted* like he cared. He mirrored my emotions and responded with just enough warmth to make me believe it was real. Over time, I realized it was all a performance. Everything was scripted to draw me in and secure his spot in my heart. Once he had that, the mask slipped. And what I saw underneath was cold and calculated. I remember breaking down in the living room one night, crying over something cruel he had just said. He just stood there… staring. No comfort, no concern. Just a cold, empty glare that pierced through me. That moment broke something in me. It was when I realized I had bonded with him deeply, but he had never truly bonded with me.

He never felt bad for what he put me through. In fact, I started to believe he *enjoyed* having that kind of power over me. When you're dealing with a narcissist, they don't just lack empathy; they are **indifferent** to your suffering. That's what gives them the upper hand. They stay emotionally detached while you fall apart. Furthermore, let me be clear: if you're hoping they'll one day wake up and start caring…you're wasting precious time. They won't and they never will.

He Needed Admiration and Validation—Constantly
This man was never satisfied. No matter how much praise or support I gave, it was never enough. He lived off validation as if it were oxygen. Every compliment and every nod of approval fueled him, and when it wasn't there, his entire mood shifted. The worst part was that he didn't just need validation from me. He needed it from strangers, friends, and especially other women. I would be standing right next to him, and he'd go out of his way to ask another woman's opinion on something as simple as a shirt he was thinking about buying, as if I wasn't even there. As if I didn't matter in that moment. I became invisible while he soaked in the attention. And yes, I'm ashamed to say—I got used to it. I normalized the disrespect because I was too emotionally invested. He would stage moments to get attention. For example, he would get all dressed up to look like he had it all together, then post carefully crafted social media updates about his accomplishments. If he didn't get enough likes, *HE* would be upset for the rest of the day! If I didn't give him the right amount of praise, *WE* would be arguing by nightfall.

It was mentally exhausting. I couldn't even breathe without thinking about how to make *him* feel better, how to keep *him* from spiraling. I started having migraines. I was worn down. But even then, I knew telling him wouldn't matter. Why? Because he didn't care. Not really. Not about me. Just about how I made him look and feel.

Controlling Behavior and Manipulation

In the beginning, I felt seen, heard, and adored. My needs were not just met—they were anticipated. That's the trap of the love bombing phase. It pulls you in with so much intensity, you start to believe you've finally found someone who *gets you*. But three months in, things shifted. Subtly at first. Then, all at once. Suddenly, everything in the relationship was about **his** needs. Every interaction was on his terms. And nowhere was this clearer than in the bedroom. At first, he was attentive. Loving. Romantic. The intimacy we shared felt passionate and mutual, like he genuinely cared about my pleasure and experience. However, as time went on, that tenderness faded. He started making comments about my weight, and not just passing remarks. They were cutting and hurtful ones. It's one thing to have someone critique you fully dressed, but standing naked, vulnerable in front of the person who once made you feel beautiful will break something inside you. For the first time in my life, I was ashamed of my body. I started hiding under oversized t-shirts during sex, just to protect myself from his judgment. And the irony? He was at least 30 pounds overweight himself, which he had gained unexpectedly since I met him at the running club. Yet his flaws were never up for discussion—only mine.

That's how narcissists control you—through criticism that chips away at your self-worth. I learned quickly that if I just went along with what he wanted, the criticism would ease up. So I did. I shrunk myself, twisted myself, and bent over backwards to keep the peace. Worse than that, he weaponized my vulnerability. All the personal things I shared with him early in the relationship, because I thought we had a real connection, were later used by him to manipulate and control me. I didn't know then that love bombing isn't just about winning your heart; it's about collecting emotional ammo. When he began threatening to expose things I'd told him in confidence, it crushed me. I turned to family for support, only to discover that I had made the mistake of turning to the *wrong* ones. Some of my family members had never really been my safe space. They were toxic, unsupportive, and envious since I was a child. And to make matters worse, they *liked* him! They saw his charm, his broken-boy routine, and fell for it. They told me

I should be more understanding, and that loving him meant staying and supporting him while he "worked through his issues." Sadly, the truth is—he wasn't working through anything. He was *working me*. He got more out of me than anyone ever had. He twisted every piece of love I gave him into a tool to control me. And I let it happen, because back then, my boundaries were too weak and my self-worth was already under attack.

His Sense of Entitlement

He walked through life like the rules didn't apply to him. Everywhere he went, he expected special treatment. Called himself a "hustler," but really, he was just a taker always looking for a shortcut, always trying to get something for nothing. With me, he never gave—only took. Furthermore, with strangers, it was the same. He'd ask for favors from people who barely knew him yet never offered anything in return. Never said thank you. Never acknowledged the emotional debt he was stacking up. He had no concept of boundaries, no respect for anyone's limits, especially if they had a kind heart. That's who he preyed on. He didn't mess with people who gave off "don't play with me" energy. No, he reserved his predatory behavior for the soft ones, the kind ones, the ones like *me*. I started seeing that pattern everywhere. I saw it in how he treated strangers, and I saw it in how he treated me. He didn't just *cross* boundaries. He bulldozed them, then acted like I was the problem for having boundaries in the first place.

He Couldn't Handle Strength in Softness

What I learned with him was that narcissists don't just seek out kind people; they seek out people they assume they can control. When they realize they can't, they unravel. If he thought you were soft or empathetic, he expected that softness to translate into compliance. The moment you stood up for yourself, it wasn't just surprising; it was offensive to him. It was like he was saying, *"How dare you have a boundary?"* Or worse: *"How dare you refuse to let me mistreat you?"*

It was especially bad when he interacted with people in the service industry. That's when his entitlement came out full force. If you were a waiter, cashier, customer service rep, or anyone in a role where you were expected to serve, he believed you *owed* him something. Additionally, if you didn't meet his expectations, he'd become cruel, dismissive, even condescending. More than once, servers actually stopped waiting on us and asked someone else to take over our table. At first, I was embarrassed. Eventually, I started silently cheering them on. Watching people refuse to accept his mistreatment gave me a strange sense of hope. It reminded me that I wasn't crazy for thinking his behavior was unacceptable. I just wasn't ready to apply that same boundary for myself yet.

He'd always leave small tips, too. That part really bothered me. He acted like the world owed him the best treatment, even when he gave the bare minimum or, worse, gave nothing at all. That's one of the defining characteristics of a narcissist: they expect everything while offering very little in return.

Fragile Ego, Sharp Tongue
He walked around like he was calm and confident, but beneath his calm exterior was an intensely fragile ego. I came to learn just how sensitive he was to any kind of critique—especially if it made him feel less than perfect.

Early in the relationship, I made the mistake of expressing concern about his health. I wasn't trying to insult him; I genuinely cared. He was carrying extra weight, and I said something about it gently, from a place of love. My remark triggered him. From that moment on, he never forgot it. He didn't confront me directly that day. He waited until the time came, and he repeatedly retaliated. He started criticizing my body in ways that were cruel and personal. He'd call me names like "fat girl" and "big back." Even after I had lost weight and was struggling with body image issues already, he continued to hurl sharp words, and they stuck. It didn't matter how I looked or how I felt; he had locked me into a box in his mind, and no amount of reality could change that.

What became painfully clear was this: he could dish out criticism all day long, but he couldn't tolerate even a whisper of it in return. In his world, he was flawless. To question that, even slightly, was to commit an unpardonable offense. He needed to be seen as superior, even when the evidence said otherwise. If that meant dragging me down to preserve his inflated sense of self, so be it. He weaponized every word, every insecurity, every moment of vulnerability I ever gave him. That's how he kept control, and for a time, it worked.

Chapter 3
The Different Faces of Narcissism

As I began to truly understand narcissism, one truth became clear: not all narcissists look or act the same. Some are bold and boastful, always seeking the spotlight. Others are more subtle, quiet, calculated, and passive-aggressive. Regardless of how they present, the core is the same. Empathy is absent, there is a deep need for admiration, and a pattern of manipulation to get what they want. What makes identifying a narcissist even more difficult is that many of them mask their dysfunction behind charm, success, or acts of generosity. They don't all storm into your life like a thunderstorm. Some ease in gently, like a breeze that you don't even notice until it's knocked everything over. I've encountered several kinds of narcissists in my life, yet the one that caught me off guard the most was the covert narcissist. This person was quiet, intelligent, always the victim, and painfully hard to detect.

The Covert Narcissist: Quiet but Calculated

My uncle on my mother's side was a covert narcissist. On the surface, he seemed like a generous, polished man, an Ivy League professor, admired in his field, thoughtful enough to remember birthdays, and the one who picked up the tab at restaurants. Growing up, I thought he was someone to look up to. On the other hand, I always noticed something different between him and my mother. She never seemed especially close to him. I didn't question it then. I do now.

Everything changed during my college spring break when my uncle's wife was staying with us. She seemed fragile, withdrawn, like the light inside her had dimmed. She mainly kept to the guest room, which shared a wall with mine. I didn't know what she was running from until I heard it for myself. He called her several times, and what I overheard on one occasion shook me. He never raised his voice, but the words were sharp enough to cut. I remember him saying, "I should've never married someone who isn't as educated as I am. You're embarrassing me. You're ruining my reputation." Every comment was laced with elitism and control. He framed everything as though she had wronged him, as though he was the one being victimized. It was the first time I heard cruelty delivered so calmly. There was no yelling, no name-calling—just a slow, deliberate attempt to erode her sense of worth, one sentence at a time. If I hadn't heard it myself, I'm not sure I would've believed her. He had everyone fooled.

That's what covert narcissists do. They operate behind a mask of intellect, kindness, or refinement. In reality, beneath their mask is someone who manipulates quietly, controls emotionally, and always finds a way to become the victim. Their weapon isn't rage; it's guilt, shame, and distorted narratives. They make you question your decisions by reminding you of the disappointment *others* will feel. They'll say things like, "How could you do this to me after everything I've done for you?" or "Everyone's going to think less of you because of what you did." Suddenly, your needs and truth become secondary to their imagined suffering.

Once I saw that side of my uncle, I could never unsee it. Every visit, every family gathering, the subtle jabs and controlling energy became crystal clear. He hadn't changed; I had just learned how to recognize the manipulation for what it was. That's the danger of covert narcissists. They don't show their hand easily. However, once you recognize the pattern, it becomes impossible to ignore. It's only then that you can begin to protect yourself from it.

The Overt Narcissist: Loud, Proud, and Painfully Obvious

If covert narcissists hide in plain sight, overt narcissists walk around with a flashing sign. They are bold, charismatic, and always chasing the spotlight. On the surface, being with someone like this might seem like a thrill, full of excitement and admiration. Then, when the lights go down and the audience disappears, their true nature shows up. That was my experience. My narcissist had the attention, the voice, the presence. He could walk into a room and command it with ease. Still, as soon as we were alone—sometimes just seconds after the applause faded—he would turn cold, dismissive, and verbally abusive. Sometimes he insulted me. Other times, he tore down people we had just spent time with, mocking them behind their backs.

He needed people to like him, but he didn't actually care about them. I watched him put on a concerned face in public, only to privately say, "Who gives a f** about their issues?" He would deliver speeches that moved crowds. Afterward, he'd obsessively review his own performance, bragging about the impact he made. Meanwhile, I sat there silently, wanting to scream, "If they only knew who you really were…"

He constantly spoke about his education, his spiritual insights, and how he was "chosen" or divinely guided. If someone challenged him, he would shut them down immediately—or just walk away mid-conversation. In private, he tore me down constantly. I was either "fat" or "stupid" or both. He would yell, dismiss, and humiliate, then twist the narrative to make me feel like the problem.

He never accepted responsibility for anything. If things went well, it was because of him. If things went wrong, it was because of me. I lost my voice in that relationship. Although I wanted to leave, I couldn't. Not yet. That's the cruelty of the trauma bond. It doesn't feel like abuse—it feels like addiction. My body was chemically hooked on the highs and lows: the dopamine from his charm, the oxytocin from the rare affection, and the crushing lows when the cycle repeated. I wasn't just emotionally tied to him—I was biologically trapped.

It took near-destruction and me questioning my own will to live before I found the strength to pull away. If you're in a relationship like this, I want you to do one thing today: stand in front of a mirror. Look into your own eyes. Gaze deeply. If you don't recognize the person staring back at you, if your spirit looks dim, your posture seems defeated, and your light has faded, that's your sign. They've taken too much. You don't deserve that. One day, you'll take your power back. Start now.

The Communal Narcissist: The Hero With a Hidden Agenda

Then there's the kind of narcissist that hides behind good deeds. That's the one who seems like a saint on the outside but is manipulative and self-serving underneath. That's the communal narcissist. For example, there's a man at my church who fits this mold perfectly. He's deeply involved in community efforts—feeding the poor, organizing events, and showing up when someone is sick. From the outside, he's a dream. Behind the scenes, it's a different story. Instead of attracting people with his kindness, he actually repels them. Why? Because his generosity comes with strings attached. I've seen it firsthand. He'll hand someone a gift while saying, "You better come to my next event or this will be the last thing you get from me." His tone?

Condescending, demanding, and more like a parent scolding a child than a peer offering support.

I remember one moment clearly. He offered some women in our congregation "gifts" from his car and demanded they follow him immediately to retrieve them. The urgency and tone were completely unnecessary—especially considering they hadn't asked for anything in the first place. It was all about control. Making them jump through hoops to receive something they didn't need. And then there's the way he talks about his good deeds. One minute, he'll say, "It's no big deal," and the next, he's making sure everyone knows what he did. Either he tells you directly or arranges for someone else to announce it. It's never just about helping—it's about being seen as the helper.

His need for praise extended into giving advice, too, which was unsolicited and nonstop. He'd tell you how to raise your kids, how to behave at church, even how to dress. It was exhausting. Eventually, I realized that creating distance from him brought me peace. With narcissists like him, distance is your power. Limited contact—or no contact—isn't cold. It's healthy. Protect your energy. You don't owe anyone access to you, no matter how much they *appear* to give.

The Malignant Narcissist: Dangerous, Sadistic, and Cold-Blooded

As I mentioned before, my uncle from my mother's side was a covert narcissist. Then on my father's side, I encountered someone even darker: a malignant narcissist. Her name was Kelly, and she was my aunt. Whereas my ex was emotionally manipulative, Aunt Kelly was aggressive, bold, and flat-out dangerous. She didn't just hurt people by accident; she seemed to enjoy it. She was stunning, with piercing green eyes that could cut through you. People noticed her. And she knew it. She used her looks as a weapon, and she didn't care who got hurt in the process. In my family, it was a running joke: whenever there was a gathering, Aunt Kelly was going to curse out Uncle Charles at least twice before the night was over. And when she got angry, people scattered. When she was calm or cheerful, people flocked to her. That's the trap. This kind of narcissist will confuse you with the highs, so you tolerate the lows.

Aunt Kelly didn't live by any kind of moral code. In fact, she openly entertained relationships with men who paid her for sex even into her fifties. She would shame Uncle Charles for *not making enough money*, even though he had a solid job and provided for their home. To her, nothing was ever enough. No one was ever enough. She got off on belittling him. You could see it in her face. She'd ride him emotionally just to feel powerful. And through it all, he never stopped loving her. He stayed. And that's what hit me hardest—because I had stayed too. The trauma bond was real for both of us.

Malignant narcissists are what happens when narcissism meets antisocial behavior. They don't just lack empathy—they lack restraint. They enjoy control. They enjoy inflicting pain. They push you emotionally, sometimes physically, and they don't stop. There's no off-switch. And if you're not careful, they'll keep going until there's nothing left of you. There's something dark and magnetic about malignant narcissists. They make you feel like you're the one failing, while they quietly destroy your self-worth. You're not their partner—you're their target. Furthermore, they don't stop until they've taken everything from you: your peace, your identity, your willpower.

So if this sounds familiar and if you're with someone who controls, belittles, threatens, or emotionally assaults you, understand this: you are not weak for staying. You are in danger if you continue to. Your life, your joy, your sovereignty, they matter. Take them back before it's too late.

The Workplace Narcissist: Power Plays in the Office
Let's talk about another kind of narcissist, which is the one who waits for you at work. The one who tries to dominate you with titles, fake authority, and a constant stream of unsolicited demands. I had a coworker like that. She didn't supervise me. She wasn't my boss. Despite this, from the day I arrived, she acted like she owned me. She sent unnecessary emails, asked for reports that weren't hers to request, and inserted herself into everything I did. It got so bad that I finally asked my actual supervisor, "Do I have to report to her?" Her response was clear, "No. You only report to me." So I tried to move on. I tried to ignore her. But like most narcissists, she didn't like being ignored. Instead, the messages increased. More emails. More pressure. More attempts to dominate me.

The workplace narcissist operates by creating confusion, disrupting your workflow, and acting as if you're the problem. They try to knock you off balance, especially if they can sense your strength. If you don't push back, they escalate. If you do push back, they play victim.

Eventually, I had to draw a clear boundary. Very intentionally, I emailed her and— blind copied my supervisor. Her response? She ran to her supervisor and painted me as 'aggressive.' Suddenly, there was office gossip about me causing trouble, even though all I had done was protect my peace.

That's what they do. They gaslight. They manipulate. They bend perception to work in their favor. And the worst part is, in a work setting, you can't always walk away. You're stuck trying to survive and stay professional, while they quietly destroy your reputation and your sanity.
If you're dealing with this behavior at work, document everything. Set boundaries in writing. Keep your receipts. Most importantly, don't let them change who you are. You don't have to play their game, but you do have to protect yourself. Because narcissists don't just live in our homes—

they sit at desks next to ours. And if you're not careful, they'll turn your job into another abusive relationship.

Standing Up: How I Handled the Workplace Narcissist

I remember driving home from work one day and asking myself, "How did I get into this mess so fast? I just got here." I had only been at that job for a week. I didn't know the ropes yet, didn't know all the names, didn't know the full scope of my duties. What I did know was that I needed that job. Badly. And that made me anxious, vulnerable—and an easy target.

The truth is that narcissists are always on the hunt. Always watching and always waiting for their next target. If you're not aware of the signs, it doesn't take long before you're caught in their trap.

Narcissists in the workplace thrive off control. They carry a warped sense of entitlement and superiority. Your job, your peace of mind, your livelihood, none of that matters because they don't care about any of it. All they care about is power. If that means lying on you, overtalking you, stealing your ideas, gossiping behind your back, or creating a toxic environment where you can't breathe, they'll do it with no shame. No empathy. They're calculated. And when you finally fight back, they flip the script to make *you* look like the problem. That's precisely what happened to me.

I knew I had to do something. So, I started documenting everything. I sent emails after each negative interaction, and I copied not just my supervisor, but also hers. I did this four times in two weeks. Then, I took those emails, printed them out, attached a copy of the company's harassment and hostile workplace policies, and took them straight to HR. It was bold. Risky. I was scared I'd be labeled a troublemaker. Even so, I was done letting fear keep me silent. And just like clockwork, she responded the way most narcissists do when they realize you're done being their victim. She stopped speaking to me and launched a smear campaign behind my back.
Some folks at work believed her lies. Thankfully, many didn't.

That's the thing about narcissists—they only thrive when people stay silent. When no one holds them accountable. People know who they are. They just don't want the smoke. No longer was I avoiding the fire; I was walking through it. At that point in my life, I had just started standing up to my narcissistic ex. And this—this battle at work—became a proving ground. A place for me to practice using my voice. It wasn't just about work anymore. It was about reclaiming every part of myself that I had let others abuse. That narcissist had picked the wrong woman at the wrong time. They don't know what to do with someone who sets boundaries, speaks up, and takes *action*. Narcissists feed on fear, silence, and compliance. Take those away, and they crumble.

Eventually, that work narcissist left the company. It took longer than it should've. It always does with people like that. They hang around, wreaking havoc, while good people try to keep the peace. Nevertheless, she finally crossed the wrong person one too many times. And just like that—she was gone. I'm not gonna lie, part of me wishes it had been my complaint that got her fired. I'll take the win regardless because what matters most is that I fought back. I stood tall. And I realized I had more power than I ever gave myself credit for. That's how you start to heal—by standing up for yourself, even when your knees are shaking.

Parental Narcissist

My romantic relationship with a narcissist was painful, but the wounds didn't begin there. They started long before then with my mother. It took me years to realize that the relationship I had with her wasn't just complicated, it was deeply toxic. Only in adulthood did I come to understand that she was a narcissist, too.

Growing up, my mother had an unshakable grip on my life. She was stunning, much like her sister, my Aunt Kelly. My mother's presence was commanding, and she knew it. In fact, she and my aunt resembled each other in both appearance and energy. I started my menstrual cycle at ten, and instead of supporting me through that sensitive transition, my mother made me feel ashamed. She implied that something was wrong with my body and told me I needed to be extra kind and agreeable if I ever wanted people to accept me. That message stayed with me, and it chipped away at my confidence. If it weren't for those early messages, I believe I would've grown into a stronger, more self-assured young woman. I probably would have avoided falling into the kinds of relationships I ended up entertaining later in life. My mother would enter my room uninvited, say whatever she pleased, and show no regard for my boundaries. She called me names like "fat" and would joke that maybe I wasn't even her daughter because I didn't look like her. When I had boyfriends in high school, she would flirt with them, often wearing revealing clothing and drawing attention to herself in inappropriate ways. It was confusing and humiliating. Any success I had, like good grades, parts in school plays, and awards, was met with backhanded remarks. She never acknowledged my efforts directly. Yet, she had no problem bragging about my accomplishments to her friends. It wasn't about me succeeding; it was about how my success reflected on *her*. Her words followed me into adulthood, especially when it came to public speaking. "You better not mess up. People will never forget." I hadn't even considered failure until she planted the idea. That kind of pressure can haunt a child, and for me, it did. I've often wondered just how far I might've gone if someone had simply been in my corner.

What I felt from my mother wasn't love. It was a competition, and it was a contest I could never win. As a child, you don't have the emotional or mental capacity to match the manipulations of a parent who uses their power to control and belittle. She knew how to leverage her position, and she did. Because of her, I learned how to doubt myself. I became a people-pleaser, a perfectionist. I carried around feelings of unworthiness and confusion about what love was supposed to feel like. Therapy became a necessary part of my healing first because of her, and then again because of my ex. Eventually, I had to make the most difficult decision of all: to go no contact. I don't know how she's doing now. And I'm not sure I ever will. But what I do know is that cutting ties gave me the space I needed to start breathing again. To begin rebuilding myself. And to finally start healing from the damage done.

Chapter 4
How My Narcissist Affected Me

The Psychological, Emotional, and Physical Toll
Narcissists don't just wound the heart. They confuse the mind, silence the spirit, and leave scars that aren't always visible. The damage they do goes far beyond an argument or a cold shoulder; they distort your sense of self, reroute your path, and sometimes, make you forget why you were here in the first place. Looking back, I now see how narcissism didn't just disrupt my peace—it completely interrupted my purpose. I spent so much time and energy surviving emotionally toxic relationships that I lost sight of who I was and what I was meant to do. When you're constantly in a state of emotional defense, your brain can't focus on growth, creativity, or calling. You're not living; you're just surviving. In addition, you can't build a destiny from survival mode.

I was always on edge, constantly anticipating the next verbal jab or emotional ambush. My nervous system never rested. I lived in a state of hypervigilance, and my body responded accordingly. My heart raced more than it should have. My chest was tight most days. My sleep was light and broken. The unrelenting stress triggered the release of cortisol and adrenaline, flooding my system with anxiety and dread. It was as if my body had decided it was under attack—and truthfully, it was. I began to second-guess everything about myself. I overthought, rechecked, and worried about everything. I questioned my instincts and began to doubt my own judgment. That kind of mental erosion doesn't happen overnight—it's slow, subtle, and deeply damaging. And it was fueled by constant criticism, gaslighting, and rejection.

Even more alarming was the way my emotional pain started showing up as physical pain. I had body aches I couldn't explain. I felt exhausted even when I rested. Doctors ran tests but found nothing wrong. That's when I started to understand what trauma and emotional abuse can do to the brain. Studies show that emotional pain activates the same regions of the brain that process physical pain—specifically the anterior insula and anterior cingulate cortex. Rejection and humiliation don't just "hurt your feelings," they literally hurt your body. The amygdala, our fear center, stays activated in toxic relationships. When it does, it triggers stress responses that disrupt your immune system, digestion, memory, sleep, and more. I used to believe that phrase: "Sticks and stones may break my bones, but words will never hurt me." Now I know better. That's a lie. Words can deeply wound. Consequently, it's never "just a joke" if it hurts you. That's why your emotional safety matters more than their intentions. If someone consistently makes you feel less-than, anxious, or afraid, even if they claim it's love, it's not healthy. It's not safe.

I ignored my body for a long time. I brushed off the anxiety, the pain, the exhaustion. I kept showing up and staying loyal to someone who was draining me dry. But my body never stopped trying to warn me. Eventually, it began to break down under the pressure I refused to relieve. If you're in something similar, let this be your reminder: You are not imagining it. Emotional abuse has physical consequences. Your body is on your side, and it wants you to be safe, free, and whole again.

The Lingering Effects and Familiarity with Abuse
From the outside, I looked healthy, strong, and even. I had the kind of presence that turned heads. I was well built, womanly in stature, and carried myself in a way that suggested confidence. Yet inside, I was still unraveling

from years of psychological damage. What people couldn't see was the chronic pain, migraines, shoulder tension, aching joints, and the mental fog that came from constantly being in emotional distress.

My mother trained me to feel small. She conditioned me to doubt my worth and rely entirely on her opinions for validation. I had no idea how beautiful or capable I truly was. In high school, I walked the halls like I was average, even though there was nothing average about me. When someone showed interest in me, I questioned their judgment instead of seeing my own value. I thought I was lucky to have a boyfriend. Instead, maybe they were the lucky ones.

Everything began to shift when I left for college. Away from my mother's grip, I started to heal. I played volleyball. I joined clubs. I excelled academically. And I noticed something: if I didn't call my mother, she wouldn't call me. That's when I realized our relationship had always been one-sided. As my sense of self grew, so did her attempts to reel me back in. But I resisted. I took summer jobs and joined programs that allowed me to stay in my college town, only returning home briefly. I was intentionally building distance.

One day, I said out loud to myself, "I'm never going back to the way things were." I cried when I said it, which resulted in tears of relief, of liberation, of self-ownership. I thought I was finally done with narcissists. However, I wasn't. Because once you escape one, another is often waiting in the wings, and sometimes in a new form. It might not be a parent this time; it could be a partner. Narcissists are drawn to people who are kind, empathetic, and loyal. I had an abundance of these traits. The pain I'd endured in the past made me deeply compassionate, but that compassion made me a magnet for predators. I didn't recognize the red flags with the next narcissist. I ignored the manipulation and the subtle digs because that behavior was familiar to me. Familiarity is dangerous when your baseline for relationships has been shaped by trauma. When your nervous system is used to emotional chaos, you don't always spot it when it shows up again. It feels normal. That's how they get in.

I realized that I had developed an unhealthy tolerance for mistreatment. I laughed at jokes that hurt my feelings. I brushed off passive-aggressive comments about my thinning hair. Because my threshold for emotional pain had been set way too high by the people who were supposed to love me, I tolerated disrespect. It took time and therapy for me to learn that just because something is familiar doesn't mean it's safe. In fact, sometimes the most dangerous situations are the ones that feel eerily comfortable.

If you've been in a narcissistic relationship, be aware of this pattern. Be honest about what feels "normal" to you, and question whether that version of normal is rooted in pain. Because healing doesn't just mean walking away from the last narcissist, it means learning to recognize and reject the next one before they ever get the chance to attach.

Chapter 5
Recognizing the Red Flags

The Early Warning Signs in Relationships (Family, Friendship, Work, Romantic)

One of the most powerful lessons I've learned is this: **you can't afford to ignore the signs.** Red flags aren't random. They're patterns and early signals meant to protect you before the damage is done. But when you've grown up around dysfunction, those warnings can feel familiar. Even comforting; that's exactly how you get caught. I've been in more than one toxic relationship because I didn't recognize what was happening until I was too deep in. Now I know that **you never rush a relationship.** Whether it's romantic, professional, or family-related, time is your friend. And if someone is trying to speed things up, pay attention. That's the first move of a narcissist.

Love bombing feels like a fairytale at first, involving intense compliments, constant attention, and over-the-top gestures. Except it's a trap. It's a setup to create dependency before you realize you're being controlled. When someone sweeps you off your feet, you're not walking anymore. They're the ones steering. That's precisely where a narcissist wants you—**off-balance and vulnerable.**

Family Red Flags

When it comes to family, the signs often show up early, but we don't see them for what they are. Why? Because we're raised in it. The dysfunction is normalized. You're told that "family is everything," even when some of those family members are emotionally dangerous. If you've ever felt dread walking into a family gathering, that's not something to ignore. Narcissistic relatives isolate, criticize, and manipulate often in front of others, masked as jokes or "tough love." Always trust your gut. **If someone in your family consistently makes you feel small, it's intentional.**

Sometimes, that disdain goes back to childhood, before you were even old enough to understand it. They form alliances, play favorites, and build their status in the family by diminishing yours. You might hear phrases like, "We're just trying to help you," but the truth is, **if someone makes you feel like an outsider in your own family, they've chosen that role for you.** Let this land: **just because someone shares your blood doesn't mean they deserve your trust.** If a family member makes you feel unsafe, unseen, or unworthy, it's not on you to fix it. It's on you to protect yourself.

Friendship Red Flags

I had a high school friend who did more emotional damage to me than anyone else at that point in my life. I was quiet, a little insecure, and just grateful to have someone who paid attention to me. She was loud, confident, and surrounded by other people, and she chose me. I felt special.

Even so, here's the truth: **it wasn't a friendship. It was an emotional transaction.** We always did what she wanted. She dumped all her problems on me, but never had time for mine. When I tried to open up, she'd shut it down or change the subject. Then came the social shift. People started treating me differently. I experienced cold shoulders, strange glances, and whispers I wasn't supposed to hear. Eventually, I realized what had happened: she was talking about me behind my back. Spreading rumors, sharing secrets, lying to make herself look like the sweet, misunderstood friend, while I took the hit.

Narcissistic friends do that. They're charming in public and cruel in private. If you're the only person who seems to be misunderstood or excluded, **start questioning who benefits from that narrative.** When I stopped talking to her, the noise stopped too. That's when I knew: she had been the one poisoning my name all along.

Workplace Red Flags

Workplace narcissists are strategic and aggressive. They always target new energy. They look for people who are competent, grounded, and maybe a little unsure of themselves. Their mission? Tear you down before you gain traction.

They criticize everything you do, often under the guise of "helping." They withhold information during training, then blame you for not knowing. They encourage imposter syndrome on purpose. Because if you feel unqualified, they stay in control.

They blur boundaries, expect you to work overtime without acknowledgment, and twist every success into their own. When you mess up, and we all do, they magnify it and gossip about it. They want you isolated. They want you gone. Conversely, here's the thing: **they can only win if you stay silent.**

Final Thought: If it doesn't feel right, it probably isn't. Trust your intuition. Don't explain away discomfort. Red flags aren't misunderstandings. They're warnings from your nervous system. Listen.

Romantic Red Flags & Narcissist Tactics

Early Warning Signs in Romantic Relationships

When you first meet a narcissist, they seem perfect—**too perfect.** It's intentional. They show up like they've been tailored to your soul: same hobbies, same shows, same values. What you're really meeting is an image of you with **a performance designed to reflect everything you love, so you let your guard down.** That's what happened to me. He liked everything I liked. Talked like me. Thought like me. It felt like fate. But no one is meant to **complete** you; they're meant to **complement** who you already are. I ignored the feeling that something was off because everything seemed so right, except that the cracks showed early. Whenever I had an issue, he'd dismiss it. When I brought up something painful, he'd compare it to his own life and say, *"I wish I had your problems."* That stung.

Repeatedly. My pain never had a place in the relationship because his always took center stage. There was also that moment when I kindly corrected him, but his reaction was explosive. Over-the-top anger. That should have been my wake-up call. That kind of temper isn't a one-time thing. It's a **preview.**

Another red flag? He was eager to meet my family and friends at first. However, once he met them, he began pulling me away from them. Suddenly, he didn't like them. Consequently, I was spending less time with people who knew and loved me. And the strangest part? **I never met his family.** He knew my people, but I didn't know his. That imbalance should've screamed danger.

The Tactics Narcissists Use to Gain Control
Narcissists manipulate perception to maintain control. One of the most common and clever ways they do this is by "turning the crowd against you." They create the illusion that everyone is rooting for your relationship. Furthermore, your friends, your family, and even strangers think you're lucky to have them, which is rarely the truth. Often, people wonder why you're still in it.

That illusion of public expectation was a trap for me. I didn't want to look weak. I didn't want to seem like I couldn't hold a relationship together. So I stayed even when I was miserable.

Narcissists are obsessed with image. And when you're with them, they force you into becoming part of that image. He couldn't stand the thought of looking bad in public, and that anxiety bled into me. I became obsessed with looking like I had it all together, too. My people-pleasing came roaring back, stronger than ever, just like it did when I lived under my mother's shadow.

Abandonment

He would leave me—just up and go. Somehow, I'd find myself apologizing to him just to get him to come back, even when I had done nothing wrong. The relationship became a cycle of rejection, return, and regret. **He trained me to beg for what I already deserved.** That's what narcissists do. They don't just hurt you—they rewire you. They isolate you from your voice, your power, your purpose. And the more disconnected you become from who you are, the easier it is for them to move in and take over.

Eventually, I didn't even recognize myself. I was emotionally enslaved, doubting everything about my worth and identity. He had wrapped himself so tightly around my mind that I couldn't imagine surviving without him. **But I did.**

Trusting My Gut

One of the most vital lessons I've learned is this: **your body knows.** Long before your mind catches up, your nervous system is trying to protect you. We are born with internal warning systems—subtle yet powerful cues designed to keep us safe. But when we've been conditioned to ignore them, especially in toxic relationships, we start losing our ability to trust ourselves.

Think about it—have you ever stood in line at the grocery store and suddenly felt like someone was standing too close? You turn, and sure enough, someone's in your personal space. That sensation? That's your **biofield** at work. The heart emits an electromagnetic signal that can extend several feet beyond your body. It's part of how we pick up on what's around us—physically, emotionally, energetically. That same system alerts us when something or someone is emotionally unsafe. The tone of a voice, a facial expression, an offhand comment—it can trigger something deep inside that says, *"You're not safe here."* The challenge is that many of us have been trained to **ignore those signals**, especially when the threat is coming from someone we care about.

That's exactly what happened to me. About three months into the relationship, the mask came off. The love bombing ended, and the criticism, gaslighting, and emotional manipulation began. My body knew before I did. I became anxious, nervous, and constantly on edge. Instead of pulling back, I leaned in. I stayed. And in staying, I silenced the one voice that had always tried to protect me: **my own.** Over time, he didn't have to work as hard to control me; I was doing it to myself. I had stopped listening to my inner voice. What I've come to understand is that when we ignore our gut, three things begin to happen— **resistance, confusion, and then resignation.**

At first, your body resists. The alarms get louder. You feel panicked, unsettled, hyper-alert. Consequently, when you don't act, when you stay, the brain and body get confused. They interpret your inaction as a signal that the threat may not be real. The warning system adjusts, not because things are safe, but because it assumes your lack of response means it overreacted. Eventually, the signals dull. You stop feeling alarmed. You start feeling numb. **Yet the danger hasn't gone away—you've just adapted to it.** This is what makes it so difficult to leave. Not because you don't want to, but because you've been rewired to normalize the very thing that's hurting you.

Eventually, though, I reached my limit. I was exhausted physically, emotionally, and spiritually. That's when I started hearing the signals again. That's when I finally listened. And that's when I began to leave. It took time. It took strength. Most of all, it took **reconnecting with my own inner voice.** The voice that said: *You're not crazy. You're not weak. You're not overreacting. You're just in danger—and you need to get out.*

If I could offer you just one piece of advice, it would be this: **trust your gut the first time it speaks.** It's not just a feeling. It's your soul trying to protect your future.

Chapter 6
I Tried to Avoid Setting Boundaries With My Narcissist

You Don't Have a Choice—You Have to Set Boundaries
For the longest time, I avoided setting boundaries with my narcissist. It wasn't because I didn't need to, but because I was afraid. Deep down, I was scared of what would happen if I stood up for myself. He never hit me, but the emotional intensity, the intimidation, the looming threat of his reactions were all quite enough to keep me quiet. I constantly worried about how he'd respond if I did what was best for me. Would he yell? Belittle me? Twist the story and turn everyone against me like he always threatened to? The truth is, I was terrified. He managed to be even more cruel, more dismissive, more damaging than my own mother—and that says a lot.

Then something happened. I got the flu. For three days, I was completely out of it. I was bedridden, worn down, and unable to do anything. It was probably my body waving a white flag from all the stress and emotional chaos I'd been enduring. On the third day, just as I started feeling a little better, he came home and walked straight into the bedroom.

Without a second of compassion or care, he looked at me and said, *You big, fat, lazy, fat, dumb, fat bitch."* Over dishes! That's what set him off. And just like that, something inside me broke. Or maybe it **woke up.** I didn't say anything right then, but something in me shifted. Something ancient. Something powerful. Later that evening, I did something I had never done before: **I wrote down a boundary.**

"I will not allow him to call me names ever again. If he does, I will start packing my bags—immediately."

That was the beginning. It might not sound like much, but for me, it was everything. I felt a surge of power return to me—like a part of me had been waiting for this moment all along. This wasn't just a promise. It was a declaration.

Boundaries Must Be Written—and Enforced

I quickly learned something profound: **writing it down changes everything.** Putting your boundaries on paper transforms them from fleeting thoughts to sacred vows. It's no longer just a hope—it becomes a plan. So I kept writing. Next, I wrote: *"I will no longer give him my paycheck."* Yep. I had been handing over my entire paycheck and letting him handle all of our finances. Turns out, while our bills went unpaid and my car sat with bald tires, he was using my money to spoil another woman. She got new tires, oil changes, and a sound system. All while I was riding dirty and emotionally bankrupt. So I wrote it all down, and I kept reading it—over and over—until I believed I had the strength to do something about it.

Then one night, he called me a "dumb mf" because I left a light on overnight. That was it. I stared at him. No yelling. No crying. Just clarity. I walked into the bedroom, opened the closet, and started packing. He had gone downstairs, clueless. I hadn't told him about my boundary. I didn't need to. **I was about to show him.** Within 30 minutes, two suitcases were in the car. He only realized what was happening when he heard the front door slam. I saw him standing in the front yard as I drove off—frozen. Confused. I watched him in my rearview mirror like a ghost I was finally done chasing. And I felt free. For the first time in that relationship, I had followed through. Not just with words, not just in my head—**but in real life.** And that made all the difference.

Manipulation and Backlash Will Come Once You Set Boundaries

Setting boundaries with a narcissist isn't a quiet or easy process—it's a war. The moment you stand up for yourself, expect a storm. There will be backlash. Insults. Accusations. Maybe even threats. Narcissists don't respond to boundaries with respect—they react with rage, manipulation, and intimidation. You've given them control for so long that your sudden independence feels like betrayal. To them, it's not just disobedience—it's **disrespect.** So what do they do? They start the smear campaign. They rewrite the story so that **you** are the villain—the unstable one, the ungrateful one, the selfish one. They'll twist the facts, distort the past, and do everything in their power to make others believe that **you** ruined everything. It's brutal, and it's intentional. Their goal? To isolate you, shame you, and break you down enough that you come crawling back. That's what happened to me.

At first, my narcissist lashed out with words that would make your skin crawl. He said things I wouldn't say to my worst enemy. However, once he realized his aggression wasn't working, he switched tactics. Suddenly, he was soft.

Reflective. He tried to get me to feel sorry for him. This is classic **emotional manipulation.** When rage fails, they shift into sympathy. He started talking about the "good times," the "chemistry," how we "just needed to work on things." He sounded sincere. For a split second, I almost believed him, but I didn't go back, because by then, I was awake. I had finally had enough. So when that failed too, he tried to rewrite the entire relationship. Now he was the victim. Now he was the one who had been misunderstood. He told me *I* was the problem. *I* didn't follow his "rules." *I* didn't show him love the way *he* needed. He actually said, "You hurt me every time you didn't do what I asked, because my love language is acts of service." Can you believe that? He took Gary Chapman's *The 5 Love Languages* and twisted it into a tool of control. He tried to weaponize a book about connection and turn it into a checklist for obedience.

That's what narcissists do. They hijack healthy tools like therapy, communication, self-help language, and use them to manipulate and gaslight. If they go to therapy, it's not to heal. It's to gather intel. Even my therapist warned me: couples therapy with a narcissist can backfire. It gives them more tools to hurt you. Luckily, none of it worked. I was done, really done. I had lost myself in that relationship. I didn't know who I was anymore. I wasn't free, and I had to take action. Setting boundaries didn't just protect me—it **freed me.** No. **I** freed myself. And from that moment forward, I made a promise to myself:

    I will be the one to keep myself safe.
    I will be the one to protect my peace.

No one else gets that job but me.

Chapter 7
How to Communicate with a Narcissist

Detached and Strategic Communication is an Art
Just because I finally left my narcissist didn't mean I was done dealing with him. We still had unfinished business. There was the shared property, joint assets, and legal ties that had to be untangled. Although I was out of the relationship, I wasn't about to let him walk away with everything we built. That wasn't happening. So, I had to figure out how to communicate with someone who specialized in emotional warfare. I couldn't go into this unarmed. I had to have a plan. No more emotional conversations. No more open-ended calls. No more giving him chances to twist my words or play on my heart. This had to be business. Strictly business.

So I wrote out a strategy.
- *Keep every conversation under five minutes*
- *Don't engage in small talk*
- *Stick to facts*
- *End the conversation—don't wait for his approval*
- *Hang up if he gets out of line*

I rehearsed those scenarios as if I were preparing for a courtroom trial. Because with a narcissist, you are always on trial. The only way I could avoid slipping back into that submissive, emotionally drained version of myself was by scripting my boundaries in advance. And for the first time in the relationship, I put **myself** first.

I Had to Use the Gray Rock Method
The hardest part? Staying calm. This man had trained me to be apologetic and soft-spoken. I had spent so much time walking on eggshells that I forgot what solid ground felt like, and that was over. I needed a new approach, one that would keep me from spiraling every time we talked. That's when my therapist introduced me to the **Gray Rock Method**.

The concept is simple but powerful: Become boring. Emotionless. Unshakable. Give bland, neutral responses. Don't feed the drama. Don't give him the reaction he's used to getting from you. At first, I thought, *"There's no way I can do this."* He knew every button to press, every weakness to exploit. Then I realized I must practice. I rehearsed my tone. I visualized staying calm no matter what he said.

- I started meditating daily
- Journaling my thoughts
- Practicing mindfulness
- Feeding myself affirmations

These were my emotional weights in the gym. They strengthened my ability to stay steady when he tried to throw me off. And guess what? It worked. The first time I used gray rock on him, he lost it. He was furious. He called me names, tried to bait me into a fight, and talked trash about my family, but I didn't budge. I didn't flinch. I didn't give him what he wanted. I just **watched** him unravel. It felt like reclaiming every piece of my power he ever tried to steal. When I felt myself getting triggered, I didn't argue. I simply said, "The movers will be here tomorrow," and I left the house. That was it! That was growth! That was power!

Understanding Reactive Abuse and Brain Damage
Here's something nobody tells you: when you finally react to all the abuse you've endured, they'll call *you* the abuser. It's called **reactive abuse**. After months or years of emotional torment, you snap—yell, cry, break down—and suddenly, *you're the problem.* Suddenly, *you're unstable.*

They'll say, "You need help," while completely ignoring what they've done to push you there. Don't fall for it. That's part of the manipulation.

I used to believe my narcissist when he said I was overreacting or I was "too emotional." Yet I learned that reacting to abuse is not a flaw—it's **self-defense.** Long-term emotional abuse doesn't just hurt your feelings. It literally damages your brain. It alters how your mind regulates emotions and processes danger. For me, that realization hit deep. It made me think back to my childhood, particularly to my mother, and all the moments with her that I felt small, invisible, and unwanted.

How much of my trauma started long before he came along? That's the thing about healing. When you leave a narcissist, you're not just walking away from a bad relationship. You're starting a full-scale recovery mission. You're healing the childhood wounds that made you tolerate the abuse. You're repairing the trust you lost in yourself. You're rebuilding your brain, your peace, and your identity—**from the inside out.**

I Started Avoiding Emotional Conversations and Power Struggles

One thing I had to learn the hard way: **you cannot win a power struggle with a narcissist.**

Why? Because they don't fight to solve—they fight to control. My narcissist was a master of turning nothing into something. A misplaced word, a different phrase, a tone he didn't like, or anything he could conjure to spark a fight. If I called the couch a "sofa," he'd argue that it was called a couch, not a sofa, and suddenly, we were in a 45-minute debate over semantics. This was his game. This was how he kept me engaged, distracted, and drained. I was exhausted all the time, not because life was hard, but because he made it hard **on purpose.**

When I finally decided to leave, I began to notice these patterns with a sharper eye. I could feel how addicted he was to control. So I changed my approach. Instead of explaining myself, I started saying:
- "Okay."
- "I see."
- "You're right."

Just those simple words. Short. Dry. Emotionless. He hated it. Why? Because it **starved him.** Narcissists feed off your reactions. Your energy is their fuel. When you stop giving it to them, you become useless to them. Consequently, when a narcissist can't use you, they lose interest in you, but not before they lash out and try to regain control.

Those one-word answers were my shield. They cut the oxygen to his fire. Every time I didn't engage, it frustrated him more. He started working overtime to provoke me, but I had already learned the truth: **silence can be stronger than shouting,** especially when it's intentional.

Now I'd be lying if I said that once I left, I was all good. The freedom didn't come without pain. Once the chaos was gone, the trauma showed up. Loud. Heavy. Constant. I had escaped the relationship, but I hadn't escaped what the relationship **did** to me. It introduced a kind of damage I didn't know how to heal. And I was about to learn that leaving a narcissist is not the end of the story. **It's the beginning of your healing journey.**

Chapter 8
It Was Time for Me to Go

The Warning Signs Were Loud—and Getting Louder
When you're in a relationship with a narcissist, the signs that something is deeply wrong are always there. You just become skilled at minimizing them. Some signs are small and silent, others shake your body like thunder, but they all point to the same truth: **you are not safe here.** At first, I ignored the signs. I told myself I was adjusting. As time went on, the damage became physical. I began experiencing stress-related symptoms I'd never had before, such as migraines, irregular periods, tremors, and unexplained weight changes. My nervous system was in a constant state of high alert. I was being drained on a biochemical level.

I remember the first irregular period as if it just happened. My cycle had always been regular, but six months in, while the gaslighting and emotional abuse were ramping up, my body sent out its first cry for help. I didn't realize it then, but my body knew before my mind did: *This is not a safe space. This is not a time for nurturing. This is not a place for creation. This is survival mode.* The clearest signal, the one I couldn't ignore, was the darkness that crept into my thoughts. I began imagining an escape that was far too permanent. I was in what I now call a **"suicide mind."** In that fog, I did something I never thought I'd do: I threw myself down the stairs. On the way down, I changed my mind. I survived and only suffered from a broken arm. As I lay there in pain, I made a promise to myself: *I have to get out of this. I have to leave him, or I won't survive.*

I Was Terrified to Leave—But I Did It Anyway
Even with every warning sign screaming at me, leaving wasn't easy. Why? Because I was convinced I couldn't live without him. That belief had been planted in me—watered by manipulation, reinforced by isolation, and kept alive by fear.

That's the thing about narcissistic abuse: it doesn't just trap you emotionally; it rewires you. I was trauma-bonded. Addicted to the highs and lows, the confusion, and the crumbs of affection. He had created an emotional addiction I didn't know how to break, so I started making small shifts. I began reframing his behavior. The kind gestures I once called "love"? I started seeing them as **strategies.** The withdrawal I felt when I tried to pull away. I started seeing it as **temporary.** And the pain? I started noticing that as **part of the healing.** I focused on where I wanted to go, not on what I was leaving behind. Slowly, the trauma bond began to weaken.

Fear of Retaliation Is Real

I'd be lying if I said I wasn't afraid of what he might do.
- He had lied about me before
- Spread rumors that I had a drinking problem
- Turned mutual friends against me
- Controlled our finances
- Threatened to ruin me

I didn't know what his next move would be, and I didn't underestimate him. Fear kept me stuck for longer than I care to admit, but once I decided to leave, I got serious about protecting myself.
- I started documenting everything
- Recording what I could
- Lying about my financial situation just enough to build some savings
- Learning how to file restraining orders
- Gathering evidence

- Preparing for the worst, just in case

Every action I took helped me reclaim my power, no matter how small. Piece by piece, I built a path out of the darkness. When I finally walked away, I knew without a doubt: **I didn't just leave him. I saved my own life.**

Chapter 9

It Took Time, but I Recovered from Narcissistic Abuse

Leaving my narcissist was not the end of the story. It was the beginning of my healing. The damage he left behind wasn't just emotional; it was spiritual, psychological, and deeply embedded in my sense of self. Even after I walked away, he lingered in my mind. I thought about him constantly. Part of me wanted to return, to make sense of the chaos, to reclaim what I thought we had, but I knew I couldn't. He had already given me unwanted gifts like anxiety, depression, trauma, and self-doubt. I couldn't afford to accept anything more from him. If I could have handed it all back, I would have. Unfortunately, that's not how this works. Narcissists rarely take back what they give. They discard and devalue. They leave you holding the weight of everything they broke.

Even so, I believed I could heal. I believed that I could restore my self-worth, rebuild my confidence, and step into a life that felt free, peaceful, and whole. I made a personal vow to construct a life that was no longer controlled by manipulation or fear.

I Had to Acknowledge the Trauma and Begin Healing

Being in a relationship with a narcissist doesn't come with the kind of challenges that healthy relationships do. You can't apply standard conflict resolution techniques when the other person is only interested in control. Narcissists aren't seeking mutual understanding; they're seeking dominance. Healing began when I finally named what I had been through. I had to tell myself the truth: I was not weak. I was traumatized.

It was not my fault that my self-esteem had been dismantled. It was the direct result of being devalued, gaslit, and emotionally manipulated. The chronic anxiety I felt—the constant state of vigilance—was not a personality flaw. It was a symptom of emotional warfare. The exhaustion I lived with wasn't laziness. It was the natural consequence of being drained over and over again by a cycle of abuse. Sometimes, daily, I had to remind myself that healing was possible., I was going to rise from this, and I was allowed to reclaim my power. Oftentimes, I had to say those things out loud to hear myself believe them.

I Resisted the Urge to Seek Closure

One of the most powerful urges I had to fight was the need for closure. I wanted one last conversation. One final goodbye. Some explanation that would make everything make sense.

I had to remind myself that closure was a fantasy. What I was really seeking was reassurance from someone who had proven they were not capable of offering anything that would lead to peace. That urge wasn't true; it was trauma speaking, and I had to find a way to silence it. Here's how I did that.

First, I accepted that he wasn't going to change. For years, I clung to the hope that one day he'd wake up, look at me, and finally see me. Finally apologize. Finally, take accountability. I dreamed about that moment, but the truth was undeniable. Every day I stayed, he chose to hurt me again, and again, and again. Why would someone so invested in power and control ever decide to change?

Second, I went no contact. After our legal matters were settled, I blocked him on every platform: social media, phone, and email. I deleted his number. I avoided places I knew he frequented. I knew I wasn't strong enough to see him unexpectedly. I had to protect my energy. I had to prioritize my healing.

Finally, I rewrote the story. Journaling became a lifeline. In those pages, I stopped romanticizing our past and started telling the truth. I wrote about the shame I felt. The panic attacks. The tears I cried in silence. The physical symptoms I endured and the way he made me feel like I didn't matter. Every time I reread those entries, I remembered why I left. Every sentence reminded me that going back wasn't an option. Eventually, the pages became proof that I was stronger than the pain.

Chapter 10
No Contact vs. Low Contact

Leaving my narcissist was one of the hardest things I've ever done, and one of the most empowering. It marked the beginning of my liberation, not just from him, but from the mental and emotional control he had over me. I knew that if I was going to stay free, I had to be intentional. I had to obliterate his power, not just from my life, but from my mind.

I worked closely with my therapist to create a strategy that would keep me from slipping back into the cycle. He recommended what's widely known as the **"No Contact Rule,"** a complete cutoff from all forms of communication. That is the most effective way to weaken the narcissist's influence, sever the trauma bond, and begin healing. However, in my situation, complete detachment wasn't possible right away. As I mentioned earlier, we still had shared property, and I wasn't going to hand over everything we built together. So I opted for what's known as **"Low Contact."**

When No Contact Isn't an Option: Mastering Low Contact

In the beginning, I couldn't completely disappear since the shared property made it impossible to go full no contact immediately. So I used the next best thing: Low Contact. This is implemented when you must interact with a narcissist due to legal ties, shared children, family relationships, or professional obligations. It is strictly business—no personal exchanges, no emotional openings. I made that very clear to him.

I Wrote Out My Boundaries—Literally

To protect myself from being pulled back in, I created a written communication plan. I wrote down exact limits:

- No phone calls longer than 5–7 minutes
- Only contact when absolutely necessary
- No personal conversations—strictly business
- No responding to jokes or light-hearted banter
- I would define when, where, and how we communicated
- Use emails and texts only—for accountability and clarity

Writing it down gave me structure. It gave me strength. When you're dealing with emotional chaos, a written plan brings order. Don't just think it—write it. The clarity that comes from seeing your boundaries in black and white is powerful.

Best Practices for Low Contact in Specific Situations

Co-Parenting with a Narcissist

- Use a parenting app to keep all communication documented
- Stick to child-related matters only—no small talk or personal check-ins
- Stay calm and neutral, even when provoked
- Meditate or ground yourself before any interaction
- Involve a third party or legal mediator whenever possible. It slows the narcissist down and limits their ability to manipulate

Dealing with Narcissistic Family Members

- Avoid gatherings held at their homes. Don't walk into their territory
- Learn how to redirect conversations. Don't give them emotional access

- Know that family members cross boundaries quickly—set yours early
- Stop expecting apologies or validation—they're not coming
- Create emotional distance, even if physical distance isn't possible

Working with a Narcissistic Boss or Colleague
- Document everything. Keep records, emails, and time-stamped notes
- Maintain professional distance—don't joke, vent, or get too familiar
- Set hard boundaries around your time and energy
- Don't let them manipulate you into overworking without compensation
- Always remember: it's just a job—your peace matters more

When I Went No Contact

Once our legal and financial entanglements were resolved, I went fully no contact, and I didn't look back. I blocked him on every platform. I avoided friends who were shared and skipped events where he might show up. Even if I received something in the mail that looked like it came from him, I tossed it without hesitation. I had to be that extreme. This was my healing, and I took it seriously.

Here's why **No Contact works**:
- It cuts off manipulation—no more gaslighting, guilt-tripping, or emotional traps
- It breaks the trauma bond—removing the stimulus allows your brain to regulate and heal
- It creates emotional clarity—you're no longer stuck in confusion and emotional chaos
- It restores your sense of self—you finally have space to focus on you

I began to think clearly again. I started to feel like *myself* again. And every day I stayed silent, I reclaimed a little more of my power.

The Emotional Challenges of No Contact

No contact is powerful, but it isn't easy. I experienced deep guilt for cutting him off, especially when he weaponized that guilt through others. A friend of his contacted me saying my narcissist told him "I was treating him like a dog." That nearly broke me, but I didn't respond. There were also days when I missed him. The emotional addiction created by the abuse cycle made some days harder than others. Of course, he didn't give up easily. He was relentless in trying to break my silence. Despite the emotional rollercoaster, I stayed the course. Though it was difficult, silence saved me.

Hoovering: How He Tried to Pull Me Back In
"Hoovering" is the narcissist's attempt to suck you back into the cycle of abuse, especially after you go no contact.

My narcissist tried *everything*!

- **Fake apologies and performative remorse**
  "I've changed," he said. "I finally understand what I did." Yet his eyes, which were often cold and manipulative, betrayed his words. I'd heard it all before. Every time I came back, he reverted to the same patterns.
- **Guilt trips and emotional blackmail**
  "After everything we've been through, you're just going to walk away?" he said. The irony. Yes, *after everything I had been through*, I was finally walking away—for good.
- **Fabricated emergencies**
  One day, I got a message from his brother, who I

didn't know well because he limited my access to his family. Supposedly, his mother was in a serious car accident, and he wanted me to come to the hospital. My gut told me something was off. I called her directly and discovered she was there for a routine checkup. This urgency was another manipulative lie.

- **The smear campaign**

    When I didn't respond, he turned to character assassination. He told anyone who would listen that I was unstable, cruel, and that *he* was the victim. That's when I learned something important: Anyone who believed his lies didn't deserve a place in my life. I cut them off, too.

- **"Love bombing" by mail**

    When everything else failed, he sent flowers. A note that reminisced about "our best memories." Earlier in my healing, this tactic might've worked. By that point, I had built enough emotional immunity to recognize manipulation when I saw it. It didn't faze me.

Final Word on No Contact

Here's the truth about the **No Contact Rule**: *It only works if you truly commit to it*. That means no responding. Not even to "one last message." Not even to "check in." If you give the narcissist any opening, they will take it and exploit it. Silence is your greatest weapon, and distance is your strongest shield. Protect your peace. Reclaim your voice; don't look back!

How I Maintained No Contact and Low Contact Successfully

Setting boundaries is one thing. *Maintaining* them takes intention and discipline. Here's what helped me stay the course:

1. I Eliminated Triggers

I blocked him on all platforms and deleted his number. I wanted no digital traces left. One month later, I got a call from an old number he once told me he no longer used. He had lied. That number was for *me*, while the other was for *her*—whomever she was. When I heard his voice, it sent my body into panic. My entire week was thrown off. That was when I realized: **half-blocking doesn't work. Go all in or not at all.**

2. I Reminded Myself Daily Why I Left

Our brains like to romanticize pain when we miss someone. This is called a **false memory, which is** a psychological trick that rewrites the past through a softer lens. To fight that, I wrote a list of every reason I walked away:

- Every lie
- Every manipulation
- Every moment I felt small
- Every day I cried
- Every time I doubted myself

That list kept me grounded when nostalgia tried to lie to me.

3. I Leaned on My Support System

I stopped isolating myself. I reached out to people who cared about me and told them the truth. Their support, their validation, and their reminders of who I was *before* the abuse helped me remember who I was becoming now.

4. I Built New Connections

New friendships helped me shift focus. I surrounded myself with energy that wasn't tied to my trauma. These fresh connections gave me room to grow, room to laugh again—and proof that *life after a narcissist* could be beautiful.

When you're dealing with someone who thrives on chaos, strategy is survival. No Contact and Low Contact are more than boundaries; they are *lifelines*. Use them. Stick to them and don't apologize for choosing peace.

From Humiliation to Healing: Reclaiming My Power
I continued journaling throughout my recovery, documenting the manipulation, the cruelty, the emotional warfare I endured. My journal became a lifeline. When moments of weakness came—and they did, I turned to the pages where I had written the truth. Not the sugar-coated memories. Not the false hope. *The truth.* One entry in particular always jolted me back to reality: the night he threw a beer in my face during a family gathering. He made it look like an accident. Everyone seemed to believe him. And worst of all, I defended him. I laughed it off in public, then cried behind closed doors. That moment was one of the lowest points in my life. It wasn't just the act, it was the way I betrayed *myself* to protect him. From that point on, I stopped calling him by name. I started referring to him as **"my narcissist."** It might seem small, but making this adjustment in how I thought of him and how I addressed him in my mind, helped me to stop romanticizing it. He

became a category, not a person. A warning label, not a memory to long for.

Surrounding Myself with Strength

One of the biggest reasons people return to narcissists is a lack of support. Isolation becomes a trap, and the narcissist becomes the only voice you hear. I knew I needed good people around me. The first person I let in was my therapist. Therapy was a game-changer. If you're recovering from narcissistic abuse, I can't stress this enough. **Get a therapist who sees you, hears you, and understands trauma.** Don't settle. You deserve to be fully understood.

For a while, I also joined a support group for survivors of narcissistic abuse. It felt good at first—I wasn't alone, and that meant everything. Eventually, I unfortunately saw many members return to their abusers. That hurt. I had to step away. Even that experience gave me fuel: it reminded me how deep the narcissist's hooks go, how easily they can reel people back in. More importantly, it made me more determined *never* to go back.

Breaking Generational Patterns

This wasn't just about him. My struggle with narcissistic relationships didn't start with him; it began at home. My mother was a narcissist. My father watched it all unfold and never stepped in. I love him, but he faded into the background of my life. He was quiet when I needed protection. And that silence shaped me. I never had a healthy model for love. Dysfunction was my baseline. I didn't know what safe felt like—until I learned the hard way what *unsafe* really was. Now I know better.

A healthy relationship makes you feel seen, valued, and safe. It allows you to grow, not shrink. You feel *expanded*, not contracted. Boundaries are respected. Your voice is heard. There's reciprocity, not exhaustion. When someone loves you in a healthy way, you don't feel drained—you feel *replenished*.

Freedom Is a Choice—I Chose Mine

Here's something I want you to remember: **you cannot heal in the presence of negative energy.** It weakens you. It opens the door for more toxicity. If you're trying to stay away from a narcissist, you *must* surround yourself with people who are good for your soul. Not just kind. Not just familiar. But *healthy*. I chose my freedom. I chose peace. And that decision gave me my life back. My narcissist drained my energy for four long years. Sometimes I wonder how much time he stole from me. Studies suggest that toxic relationships can shave 7–12 years off your life. Whether that's true or not, one thing is certain: **I will never allow anyone a chance to do this to me again.**

I protect my peace now. I honor myself. And for the first time in a long time, I feel at ease.

Chapter 11

Rebuilding My Life—One Layer at a Time

(Discernment, Healing, and the Work of Becoming Whole)
Leaving my narcissist marked a defining moment in my life. It required courage, clarity, and a level of strength I didn't know I had. Nevertheless, walking away was only the beginning. What followed was the more delicate, more sacred task of **rebuilding me**.

He had pulled me off course. I had veered far from my purpose, from my sense of self. Now I had to return to what I call my *destiny work*: the mission, the identity, the calling that had been waiting for me all along. There were wounds, yes. Deep ones. But those wounds became the soil for something new. The pain fueled my desire to create a future that was entirely my own. A future rooted in clarity, confidence, and truth. And so began the work of **self-recovery, growth, and transformation.**

Let me say this clearly: **healing is not linear.** It looks different for everyone. However, one thing is certain: healing must be intentional. I had to do more than simply *wait* to feel better. I had to *work* for it. If I hadn't, I believe I would have remained stuck in a fog of grief and confusion. But because I chose to heal on purpose, I eventually found peace.

The Grief After Freedom

Most people don't talk about the grief that follows the end of a toxic relationship. Yet, it's real. Even when the relationship was damaging, even when it hurt every single day, **grief still comes.** I had been with my narcissist for years. I had invested hope, time, dreams, and love into a future that would never exist. Letting go of that meant facing an emotional void. It felt like a contradiction of **freedom and sorrow** at the same time. I learned this: *missing someone doesn't mean they were good for you. It just means you're human.*

The Five Emotional Stages of Healing
1. Relief

The initial relief was indescribable. I felt like I had escaped a burning building. I was free. For a brief moment, the air felt clean again. Even so, that peace didn't last long—not at first. Other emotions quickly rushed in to take their place.

2. Confusion

At night, I would lie in bed and wonder, *"Did I make the right choice? Was it really that bad?"* That's what trauma does. It scrambles your clarity. Your brain becomes wired for dysfunction. Even abuse begins to feel familiar. That's why trauma bonds are so dangerous. They distort reality and create cravings for what hurt you.

3. Grief

There were nights I mourned the relationship like a death. In some ways, it was. I journaled about the loss, spoke with my therapist often, and slowly began to process what had happened. I allowed myself to cry and be honest about what I had lost and what I had *gained* by walking away. Part of this work included not just **forgiving** him, but also *myself*. Forgiving myself for not knowing, for staying too long, for believing his lies. That kind of self-forgiveness is the foundation for everything that follows. Eventually, I did forgive him; not for his sake—but for mine. Forgiveness cut the emotional cord that had tied me to him for too long. And I had to practice that forgiveness **daily**, until it finally became real.

4. Anger

Anger hit hard. I was furious about the time I had wasted, the years, the emotional labor, and the energy. I questioned how I missed the red flags. Nevertheless, I reminded myself: *he didn't show them at first*. Narcissists often appear perfectly charming, attentive, and even ideal until you're fully entangled. That's what makes them so dangerous. If you've ever asked, *How did I fall for this?* Well, you're not alone, and you are not to blame. Here's something surprising about that anger? It was necessary. It became fuel. It let me *stay away,* and eventually, it helped me *stand tall.*

5. Empowerment

As I stepped deeper into my healing, I began to remember the woman I was before I met him, and I wanted that vibrant, hopeful, strong woman back. Even more, I wanted to *become someone even wiser than before.* With guidance from my therapist, I journaled regularly. I practiced affirmations, repeating out loud:

- "I deserve peace."
- "My past doesn't define me."
- "I am worthy of joy."

I set goals and read them every day, especially when intrusive thoughts tried to drag me back into despair. I watched old movies that made me feel like *myself* again. I laughed again. I rested. I planned.

The Eight Pillars of Personal Rebuilding

My therapist encouraged me to work on eight key areas of life. These areas align us with our divine purpose and inner balance. I didn't just want to heal. I wanted to **thrive**. So, I used these eight pillars as my foundation for reconstruction, and each of these areas became part of a greater whole—*the new me.*

1. **Mental** – Cultivating emotional clarity and healthy thoughts
2. **Spiritual** – Reconnecting with God and divine truth
3. **Emotional** – Learning to regulate and express my feelings
4. **Physical** – Caring for my body through rest, movement, and nourishment
5. **Social** – Building relationships rooted in mutual respect and care
6. **Professional** – Redefining my goals and finding work that honored my worth

7. **Environmental** – Creating spaces that felt safe, sacred, and peaceful
8. **Financial** – Gaining control over money to support my independence

The Eight Dimensions of Healing

When I chose to rebuild, I knew I had to approach it holistically. Healing couldn't just be emotional; it had to reach every part of my life. These eight areas became the pillars that supported my recovery. They gave me focus. They gave me structure. And over time, they gave me back **myself.**

Mental: Clearing the Fog

The emotional and psychological abuse I experienced had left my thoughts cluttered and chaotic. One of the first gifts I gave myself was permission to feel—entirely and without judgment. Therapy played a crucial role here. It helped me name what I'd been through and understand how deeply it had impacted my thinking.

I began to create space for mental clarity. I read self-help books, journaled daily, practiced mindfulness, baked, cooked, solved puzzles, and even entertained myself with coloring books. These weren't just hobbies; they were acts of mental restoration. Over time, I began to notice something powerful: I could think clearly again. That mental fog used to control me started to lift. With it, so did my sense of direction.

Spiritual: Reclaiming the Sacred

One of the most transformative parts of my journey was rediscovering the sacredness of my own life. I started asking myself, *"What do I believe about myself?" What does God say about me?* I realized that if I had ever seen myself as sacred, I never would have allowed someone to treat me so poorly.

Growing up with a narcissistic mother had trained me to devalue myself. Now I was unlearning that. I prayed more. I meditated. I journaled. I practiced yoga. I attended community gatherings and functions. I didn't just *go to church*—I *connected* with God. And in that sacred space, I started to attract people who were just as grounded and balanced as I was becoming.

Emotional: Reclaiming My Right to Feel

During my relationship, my emotions were constantly suppressed or manipulated. I learned to smile when I was broken and stay calm when I was in distress. Healing meant reclaiming my right to feel. Through mindfulness, I learned to observe my emotions rather than be consumed by them. Instead of saying "I am anxious," I would say, "I am having thoughts that are creating anxiety." That simple shift helped me find the space between me and my feelings.

Grounding techniques became my anchor. I'd put my hand over my heart and say, "You're safe." I listened to calming music. I practiced EFT tapping, which signaled to my nervous system that I was no longer in danger. These practices helped regulate my emotions internally and gave me back a sense of safety.

Physical: Coming Home to My Body

Stress had taken a toll on my body. I ate erratically, reached for comfort food, and ignored my physical well-being. My body, like my heart, had suffered in silence. Once I left, I began to listen to my body again. I noticed how certain foods made me feel. I honored my hunger. I rested. I moved my body as gratitude, not as punishment.. I made space for facials, manicures, pedicures, and long walks. Slowly, I returned to myself emotionally and physically. There is a direct link between body and mind, and when one begins to heal, the other follows.

Social: Choosing Healthy Connections
I became intentional about who I allowed in my space. I no longer gave second chances to people who triggered me or disrupted my peace. I disconnected from toxic social media pages and instead curated a digital and personal community of inspiration, laughter, and authenticity.
Healing required healthy company. And I stopped settling for anything less.

Professional: Redefining My Worth at Work
Work used to be another area where I didn't feel seen or respected. But as I healed, I showed up differently. I set boundaries. I took breaks. I pursued training opportunities and considered new roles. That energy shift made a difference. I got promoted to project manager. For the first time, I realized that when I believe in myself and enforce healthy boundaries, *others begin to see my value, too.*

Environmental: Creating Sacred Space

During my relationship, even my home didn't feel like mine. I was too exhausted to clean. The resulting clutter added to my feelings of being overwhelmed and out of control. Once I began healing, I reclaimed my space. I cleaned with intention. I let go of clothes and items that reminded me of him—including the shirt I was wearing the day he threw beer in my face. That shirt didn't go to Goodwill. I burned it.

Decluttering became an emotional release. I created peace in my environment and noticed how much it supported my inner calm.

Financial: Taking Control, One Step at a Time

For years, money had been a mystery and a source of fear. Healing meant facing what I'd avoided. I assessed my resources. I created a budget. I canceled unnecessary subscriptions. I shopped with a list and ate at home more often—simple, powerful steps. Even with fear in the background, I chose to take control. Each small decision built my confidence. I didn't just want to survive—I wanted to thrive.

Healing Through Strategy and Intention

Addressing each of these areas helped me stop spiraling and start rising.

I learned to build what therapists called "emotional buffers," which included meditation, self-talk, mindfulness, and journaling. These are habits and routines that absorb life's shocks. These buffers gave me breathing room, mental space, and the capacity to respond rather than react. No, these changes weren't always easy, but they were always worth it. Every day I showed up for myself, I created a life that felt more like *mine*.

Chapter 12

Now That My Narcissist is Gone, I Am Healing and Thriving

Leaving my narcissist wasn't just an escape—it was a resurrection. I wasn't just surviving anymore. I was thriving. To thrive is to rise. It's to rebuild your life from the ashes with intention, wisdom, and a relentless commitment to your peace. I began using everything I'd been through as building blocks, not as baggage. The pain I endured had a purpose, and the wisdom I gained from it became the foundation for my transformation.

Turning Pain Into Power

I was no longer tolerating people, places, or things that disrupted my mental, emotional, or physical peace. I was creating a life that made sense on my terms. Healing and thriving are not the same. Healing is the quiet planning, the journaling, the therapy sessions, the setting of boundaries. Thriving is when you step on the stage of your new life and actually live out those boundaries without apology.

At first, it was hard to know which phase I was in. Then I realized if healing is the rehearsal, then thriving is the performance. Even if I had stage fright, I was ready to play the role I wrote for myself. I just needed to know how to direct the energy, the intense, raw energy left over from the trauma.

Transmuting Negative Energy

Here's the truth: negative emotions produce powerful energy. More powerful, in fact, than positive ones. Left unmanaged, that energy can break you down; however, when redirected, it can build you up. With the guidance of my therapist, I learned that negative energy doesn't have to be destructive. It can be *transformed*. Every emotion carries fuel. That heartbreak, that betrayal, that anger—it's all energy. The key is to channel it toward your growth, not your ruin.

A narcissistic relationship is not a puzzle to solve. It's a toxic system to *walk away from*. And once I walked away, I had to face the emotional residue. Suppressing it didn't work. Avoiding it made it worse. So instead, I sat with my emotions and I asked:

- What is this emotion doing to me?
- Where did it come from?
- Can I name it without shame?

This practice—mindfulness—helped me gain control over my inner world. And when the emotion was identified, I spoke to it. Out loud.

"I'm angry, but I've been angry before, and I know anger doesn't lead me anywhere good.
So I'm going to use this energy at the gym. I'm going to sweat it out.
I'm going to choose my peace."

Speaking positively out loud is one of the most effective tools in your healing. Your brain responds to your voice. That's why affirmations matter. That's why truth-telling matters. Life and death truly are in the power of the tongue. This is how I turned pain into power. The more I practiced this, the more confident I became, especially during moments of intense emotion. Even milliseconds of pause, created by speaking truth aloud, gave me time to redirect my thoughts. Eventually, I wasn't afraid of my emotions anymore. I wasn't scared of a memory, or a wave of sadness, or a flash of rage. They didn't own me. I had a command voice—and I used it.

The Calling to Help Others

As I healed, something deeper stirred inside me. It was a desire to help others heal, too. I had grown up with a narcissistic mother, and I knew what that kind of pain did to a soul. People like me usually go in one of two directions: we become narcissists ourselves, or we become deeply empathetic and mission-driven. I chose compassion. I chose purpose. Six months into my journey, I began writing this book. I joined recovery groups. I started showing up for others. The more I healed, the more compelled I felt to share what I'd learned. Not because I had it all figured out—but because I knew someone out there still felt trapped in the darkness I had escaped.

Gratitude: The Most Underrated Medicine

Gratitude saved me. Shifting my attention from what I'd lost to what I still had was nothing short of transformative. Gratitude is forward-facing. It moves you toward goodness, rather than away from pain. I practiced daily gratitude:
- I reflected on three things I was thankful for every day
- I reached out to people who supported me and told them how much they meant to me

- I joined faith groups and support communities, where understanding and empathy were abundant

Gratitude rewired my brain. Literally, it activated healing chemicals—dopamine, serotonin, norepinephrine—and shifted my mind away from fear, and toward hope. It also helped me revisit the past with new eyes. I didn't just see trauma, I saw resilience. I didn't just remember pain, I remembered survival. When we reflect on the past, we must do it with purpose. Don't stare at the wreckage. Study it. *Glean the lesson. Own the insight.* This is how we stop our past from defining us and start using it to refine us.

Gratitude Journaling: A Tool That Changes Your Brain

Writing down what I was grateful for became non-negotiable. It reduced stress. It improved my mood. It helped me catch negative thoughts and reframe them in real-time. Journaling gave me space—mental space—to see things clearly and respond instead of react. This practice activates the prefrontal cortex, the part of the brain responsible for decision-making and emotional regulation. In other words, it helps you stay grounded, even when life tries to knock you over.

Closing Thoughts

I am not just surviving. I am thriving. I am healing in public. And I am walking in purpose. I took every ounce of pain my narcissist left behind and used it to build something beautiful. I used it to build *myself*.

Let this chapter serve as your permission slip. You can be hurt and still rise. You can grieve and still grow. You can feel broken and still become whole. You have the power to turn your pain into purpose, and your purpose into peace.

Strengthening the Mind with Gratitude and Affirming Self-Talk

Trauma disrupts the brain's ability to think clearly, especially in the prefrontal cortex—our center for decision-making, emotional regulation, and rational thought. Healing that part of the brain requires intentional practice. For me, that practice was gratitude journaling. It shifted my focus from scarcity to abundance, and that simple shift fueled my motivation to keep moving forward.

Reframing My Narrative with Affirming Self-Talk

My inner dialogue needed healing just as much as my body and heart did. I began with affirmations—simple, powerful truths spoken aloud with intention. Affirmations are not just positive words; they are recalibrations. They interrupt old programming and help retrain the mind to believe in hope, strength, and worth. I had spent so long living under a cloud of self-doubt and internalized negativity, much of it reinforced by the narcissist I had left behind. But the more profound truth is this: while others may have helped shape that darkness, I had carried it, I had rehearsed it, and that meant I also had the power to let it go.

This shift started with recognizing what psychologists call **negativity bias.** This is the brain's tendency to focus more on what's wrong than what's right. When we live in this mental state for too long, everything begins to look like a threat. I used to assume the worst would happen in nearly every situation. I expected failure. I anticipated rejection, and more often than not, those assumptions became reality. That's how powerful our thinking is. When I accepted that, I also accepted that I could take my power back. I could change the lens through which I viewed myself and the world. I could train my mind to respond differently. So I did.

How I Reframed My Thinking

I started by becoming more aware of the thoughts running through my mind, especially the negative ones. Most of us have tens of thousands of thoughts every single day, and if trauma or stress has shaped our minds, many of those thoughts are self-critical or fear-based. But when I learned to *catch* a negative thought, I paused long enough to ask myself:

- Is this thought accurate?
- Is it helpful?
- Is there another way to see this?

Then I would challenge the thought by looking for a more balanced interpretation in something grounded in both truth and compassion. I reminded myself that failure didn't mean defeat. It meant data. It meant I had tried, and now I had new insight to take with me into the next attempt. That subtle shift created space in my mind for confidence to grow. Instead of saying, *"I can't believe I messed that up,"* I learned to say, *"This is part of the process. I'm learning, and next time I'll do better."* That one change shifted the entire emotional tone of my day. I felt more in control, more motivated, and less fearful of trying again.

The Words I Chose to Heal Me

I began crafting affirmations that spoke directly to my fears and answered them with courage. Every affirmation was present-tense, emotionally resonant, and intentional. For example:

- Instead of saying, *"I'm scared this won't work,"* I said, *"I trust the process, and every challenge helps me grow."*
- Instead of *"I hope I don't fail,"* I said, *"I will do my best, and I will learn no matter what."*

At first, these new phrases felt foreign, almost awkward; however, with repetition, they started to feel like mine. Over time, they became my default responses. I was literally reprogramming my brain, and I could feel it working.

There was something else I noticed, too. The more I focused on my healing, the less I thought about my narcissist. I wasn't avoiding the past; I was too engaged in the present. I was too focused on building a life worth living. This is what happens when you shift from *running away* from pain to *moving toward* your purpose.

Reclaiming My Time, My Mind, My Life
Once I understood the impact of intentional thought and self-directed focus, I became more mindful of how I spent my energy. I stopped aligning myself with people or situations that drained me. I set real goals. I wrote them down. I broke them into small steps. I gave my mind something meaningful to pursue, and that pursuit released powerful, healing chemicals in my brain: dopamine, serotonin, and endorphins. These chemicals didn't just make me feel good—they restored parts of my brain that trauma had disrupted. That's the science behind why affirming self-talk and focused goals work. They literally *heal you*. For too long, I had been on someone else's path—living according to someone else's needs, desires, and dysfunctions. But now? I was on *my* path. I was directing *my* life. And I made myself a promise: *No one will ever sidetrack me again.* If I feel my peace slipping or sense that someone is trying to hijack my journey, I step back. I regroup. I protect what I've rebuilt. Because this version of me—grounded, clear-minded, and strong—is not available for manipulation.

Combining Mindfulness with Empowering Self-Talk

Healing from narcissistic abuse isn't just about surviving the trauma; it's about restoring your relationship with your own mind. One of the most transformative tools I discovered on this journey was the fusion of **mindfulness** and **affirming self-talk**. Together, they helped me reclaim control over my thoughts, emotions, and energy.

Living in the Present: The Power of Mindfulness

Mindfulness is the art of being fully present in the moment without judgment, without overthinking, without attaching yourself to the past or fearing the future. For years, I lived outside of the present. My mind was stuck either **future-tripping** (obsessing over what might go wrong) or **ruing the past** (replaying moments of regret and betrayal). Both patterns kept me anxious, ungrounded, and depressed.

When you learn to live in the present moment, when you stop judging yourself and simply *observe* your experience, you become powerful. Why? Because the present is the only space where transformation can truly happen. You can't change yesterday. You can't control tomorrow. You can *show up* right now. Fully. Intentionally. Here's the difference: a person disconnected from mindfulness might say, *"I'm anxious right now."* Yet, a mindful person says, *"I'm experiencing thoughts and feelings that are creating anxiety."*

That second statement is powerful. It creates distance between *you* and the emotion. You're no longer the victim of anxiety; you are the **observer** of anxiety. And that shift gives you choices. You don't have to be consumed by it. You can move it. Guide it. Breathe through it. Speak to it.

This practice put me back in the driver's seat of my emotional life. My narcissist had stolen my ability to self-regulate. I had been emotionally hijacked. But mindfulness gave me back my power.

How I Used Mindfulness and Affirming Self-Talk Together

When anxiety would arise, I didn't run from it. I acknowledged it. Then I spoke to myself with truth and tenderness.

> *"I'm experiencing thoughts that are moving me toward anxiety, but I've been here before. This feeling hasn't harmed me, and it cannot destroy me.*

I choose now to guide my mind to a place of calm and grounding."

Then I'd breathe deeply. I'd close my eyes and visualize a peaceful memory—my grandfather's farm, the smell of the earth, the sun over the fields. That memory became my emotional reset button. And through that combination, **mindfulness, affirming self-talk, and visualization,** I taught my nervous system how to settle. It didn't mean I avoided difficult emotions. It meant I learned to meet them differently. I could experience anger, sadness, fear, or grief, and still remain whole. That was one of the greatest skills I gained in therapy. That was healing.

My Daily Practice: How I Reinforced the Healing
Once I understood the power of these tools, I built them into my daily routine. Every morning, I took five minutes to simply sit with myself without a phone, no distractions, just observing my emotions without judgment. I wasn't trying to "fix" anything. I was just *present*.
Then I spoke life into myself:

- *"Today is mine, and I choose to show up with peace and purpose."*

- *"You are worthy of love. You are safe. You are rebuilding something beautiful."*

If I started to feel overwhelmed during the day, I paused. I breathed. I anchored myself again.

And at night, I celebrated. I acknowledged the small wins. I reflected on how far I'd come. Even on hard days, I found something to be proud of. I wasn't ignoring pain—I was prioritizing progress. This practice rewired my perspective. Instead of asking, *"Why is this happening to me?"* I began to ask, *"What is this trying to teach me?"* And that shift brought healing.

My Moment of Realization: I Had Recovered

I can't pinpoint the exact moment it happened. Healing is subtle. Sometimes it's invisible. But one day, I looked at my life and realized something had changed.

- I was eating well
- I had boundaries that protected my peace
- I didn't allow toxic people access to me
- I had coping strategies that actually worked
- I had learned to care for myself in ways I never had before

That realization didn't come with fireworks. It came with clarity and calm. I had stewarded my life back to wellness. More importantly, I had reclaimed my power. No one could ever again control my happiness, my energy, or my identity. This is the life I was meant to live. This is the freedom I fought for.

I Healed, I Recovered, and You Can Too

It took me six years to fully recover from a relationship that lasted four. That's the truth. Sometimes, it takes longer to heal from the damage than it did to experience the damage. That's why I urge you to honor the early warning signs. When someone begins to mistreat you, believe it the first time. Don't let charm, attraction, promises, or passion distract you from what your intuition is telling you. The greatest gift you can give yourself is…*never having to recover* in the first place. If you do the work and commit to your own restoration, you will come out stronger than you ever imagined. Not just healed. Not just whole, but powerful.

If you're like me and so many others who did get caught in the web of a narcissist, then give yourself this promise:

I will not stay where I am mistreated.
I will not keep what is trying to destroy me.
I will leave, I will heal, and I will rise.

References

I. Foundational Psychology & Understanding Narcissism

- Behary, W. T. *Disarming the Narcissist*: Surviving and thriving with the self-absorbed (2nd ed.). New Harbinger Publications, (2013).
- Burgo, J. *The Narcissist You Know*: Defending yourself against extreme narcissists in an all-about-me age. Touchstone, (2015).
- Golomb, E. *Trapped in the Mirror*: Adult children of narcissists in their struggle for self. William Morrow, (1995).
- Hotchkiss, S. *Why is it Always About You?* The seven deadly sins of narcissism. Free Press, (2002).
- Malkin, C. *Rethinking Narcissism*: The bad and, surprising, good about feeling special. Harper Wave, (2015).
- Simon, G. K. *Character Disturbance*: The phenomenon of our age. Parkhurst Brothers, (2010).
- Vaknin, S. *Malignant Self-Love*: Narcissism revisited (10th ed.). Narcissus Publications, (2015).

- Goodman, C. L., & Leff, B. *The Everything Guide to Narcissistic Personality Disorder*. Adams Media, (2010).
- Thomas, D. *Narcissism: Behind the Mask*. CreateSpace Independent Publishing, (2019).
- Arabi, S. *Becoming the Narcissist's Nightmare*: How to devalue and discard the narcissist while supplying yourself. Thought Catalog Books, (2016).
- Arabi, S. *It's Not You, It's Them*: 30 days of hope and help for the adult child of a narcissistic parent. Thought Catalog Books, (2020).
- Campbell, S. *But It's Your Family*: Cutting ties with toxic family members and loving yourself in the aftermath. Morgan James Publishing, (2019).
- MacKenzie, J. *Psychopath Free*: Recovering from emotionally abusive relationships with narcissists, sociopaths, and other toxic people (Expanded ed.). Berkley, (2015).
- McKenzie, J. *Whole Again*: Healing your heart and rediscovering your authentic self after toxic relationships and emotional abuse. Berkley, (2018).

- McBride, K. *Will I Ever Be Free of You?* How to navigate a high-conflict divorce from a narcissist and heal your family. Atria Books, (2015).
- Mirza, D. *The Covert Passive-Aggressive Narcissist*: Recognizing the traits and finding healing after hidden emotional and psychological abuse. Safe Place Publishing, (2017).
- Morningstar, D. *Out of the Fog*: Moving from confusion to clarity after narcissistic abuse. Morningstar Media, (2017).
- Thomas, S. *Healing From Hidden Abuse*: A journey through the stages of recovery from psychological abuse. Southwell Press, (2016).
- Tudor, H. G. *Love and Loathing*: Recovering from a narcissist. Amazon Digital Services, (2017).
- Brown, N. W. *Children of the Self-absorbed*: A grown-up's guide to getting over narcissistic parents (2nd ed.). New Harbinger Publications, (2008).
- Cori, J. L. *The Emotionally Absent Mother*: How to recognize and heal the invisible effects of childhood emotional neglect. The Experiment, (2017).

- Forward, S. *Toxic Parents*: Overcoming their hurtful legacy and reclaiming your life. Bantam Books, (2002).
- Forward, S. & Buck, C. *Mothers Who Can't Love*: A healing guide for daughters. Harper, (2010).
- Gibson, L. C. *Adult Children of Emotionally Immature Parents*: How to heal from distant, rejecting, or self-involved parents. New Harbinger Publications, (2015).
- McBride, K. *Will I Ever Be Good Enough?* Healing the daughters of narcissistic mothers. Atria Books, (2009).
- Morrigan, D. *You're Not Crazy—It's Your Mother*: Understanding and healing for daughters of narcissistic mothers. Wormwood Publishing, (2011).
- Webb, J. & Musello, C. *Running on Empty*: Overcome your childhood emotional neglect. Morgan James Publishing, (2012).
- Adams, K. M., *Silently Seduced*: When parents make their children partners (2nd ed.). Health Communications, (2011).
- Lancer, D. *Dating, Loving, and Leaving a Narcissist*: Essential tools for improving or

leaving narcissistic and abusive relationships. Amazon Digital Services, (2014).
- Lerner, R. *The Object of My Affection is in My Reflection*: Coping with narcissists. Health Communications, (2008).
- Rosenberg, R. *The Human Magnet Syndrome*: Why we love people who hurt us? Premier Publishing, (2013).
- Simon, J. H. *How to Kill a Narcissist*: Debunking the myth of narcissism and recovering from narcissistic abuse. J.H. Simon Publishing, (2016).
- Swithin, T. *Divorcing a Narcissist*: Advice from the battlefield. Amazon Digital Services, (2013).
- Swithin, T. *The Narc Decoder*: Understanding the language of the narcissist. Amazon Digital Services, (2014).
- Zayn, C. & Dibble, K. *Narcissistic A Lovers*: How to cope, recover, and move on. New Horizon Press, (2007).
- Babiak, P. & Hare, R. D. *Snakes in Suits*: When psychopaths go to work. Harper Business, (2006).
- Cavaiola, A. & Lavender, N. *Toxic Coworkers*: How to deal with dysfunctional people on the job. New Harbinger Publications, (2000).

- Navarro, J. *Dangerous Personalities*: An FBI profiler shows you how to identify and protect yourself from harmful people. Rodale Books, (2014).
- Kets de Vries, M. F. R. *The Leader on the Couch*: A clinical approach to changing people and organizations. Jossey-Bass (2006).
- McBride, K. *My Father the Narcissist*: A story of healing. Atria Books, (2018).
- Malkin, C. *The Narcissist's Daughter*: A memoir. Harper One, (2017).
- Payson, E. *The Wizard of Oz and Other Narcissists*: Coping with the one-way relationship in work, love, and family. Julian Day Publications, (2002).
- Waite, J. *A Beautiful, Terrible Thing*: A memoir of marriage and betrayal. Plume, (2017).
- McGregor, K. *Becoming Free*: A woman's guide to internal strength. Wood Lake Publishing, (2020).
- Cloud, H. & Townsend, J. *Boundaries*: When to say yes, how to say no to take control of your life. Zondervan, (1992).
- DeGroat, C. *When Narcissism Comes to Church*: Healing your community from emotional and spiritual abuse. IVP Books, (2020).

- Johnson, D. & VanVonderen, J. *The Subtle Power of Spiritual Abuse*. Bethany House, (1991).
- Peck, M. S. *People of the Lie*: The hope for healing human evil. Touchstone (1983).
- Vernick, L. *The Emotionally Destructive Relationship*: Seeing it, stopping it, surviving it. Harvest House Publishers, (2007).

About the Author

Giovanni Bass is a retired Military Officer (Army) and a licensed clinical social worker, author, and motivational speaker dedicated to helping others reclaim their power after emotional trauma. Drawing from his own professional background in mental health and personal experiences, Giovanni writes with purpose, clarity, and compassion. His work blends psychological insight with real life strategies for healing, especially for those recovering from the manipulation, emotional damage inflicted by narcissistic relationships. Through his clinical expertise and deep empathy, Giovanni has supported many individuals on their path towards self-worth, personal transformation, and emotional balance.

In "I Chose Me," he provides a road map for those who are ready to break free from toxic relationships and rediscover themselves. When he's not writing or serving clients, Giovanni creates inspiring content on personal growth, spiritual realignment, and emotional wellness. His voice is a lifeline for survivors seeking to rebuild their lives and step fully into their power.

To connect with Giovanni Bass,
TikTok: @manifestingmindsett
IG: @manifesting_mindsett

www.ingramcontent.com/pod-product-compliance
Lightning Source LLC
Chambersburg PA
CBHW071213160426
43196CB00011B/2291